George Colman

The mountaineers

Vol. 2

George Colman

The mountaineers
Vol. 2

ISBN/EAN: 9783337717766

Printed in Europe, USA, Canada, Australia, Japan

Cover: Foto ©ninafisch / pixelio.de

More available books at **www.hansebooks.com**

THE MOUNTAINEERS;

A

PLAY,

IN THREE ACTS;

WRITTEN BY

GEORGE COLMAN;

(THE YOUNGER.)

AND FIRST PERFORMED AT THE

Theatre Royal, Haymarket,

On SATURDAY, August 3, 1793.

THE THIRD EDITION.

LONDON:

PRINTED FOR J. DEBRETT, OPPOSITE BURLINGTON-HOUSE, PICCADILLY.

1795.

ADVERTISEMENT.

SOME passages, and some few speeches, printed in the following Play, are omitted in the representation.

DRAMATIS PERSONÆ.

MEN.

OCTAVIAN,	Mr. KEMBLE.
VIROLET,	Mr. BARRYMORE.
KILMALLOCK,	Mr. JOHNSTONE.
ROQUE,	Mr. AICKIN.
MULETEERS,	Mr. BANNISTER.
	Mr. DAVIES.
	Mr. BLAND.
	Mr. BENSON.
LOPE TOCHO,	Mr. PARSONS.
PEREQUILLO,	Mr. COMERFORD.
GOATHERDS,	Mr. PALMER, Jun.
	Mr. BARRETT.
	Mr. LEDGER.
	Mr. WALDRON, Jun.
	Mr. BURTON.
BULCAZIN MULEY,	Mr. BENSLEY.
GANEM,	Mr. EVATT.
PACHA,	Mr. WEWITZER.
ALI BEG,	Mr. ABBOT.
SADI,	Mr. BANNISTER, Jun.
1st MOOR,	Mr. USHER.
2d MOOR,	Mr. COOKE.

WOMEN.

ZORAYDA,	Mrs. KEMBLE.
FLORANTHE,	Mrs. GOODALL.
AGNES,	Mrs. BLAND.

Moorish Guards, Goatherds, &c.

SCENE, SPAIN; partly in the Town and Kingdom of Granada—partly in Andalusia.

THE
MOUNTAINEERS.

ACT I.

SCENE I. *A Moorish garden in the town of Granada; at one side, the castle of Bulcazin Muley. R.—A window in one of its towers overlooking the garden. A drawbridge, leading to the castle gate.*
R.   L.   with Spades,
VIROLET and KILMALLOCK, habited as slaves, discovered at work.

KILMALLOCK.

COUNT!

VIROLET.

How now, noble captain Kilmallock!

KILMALLOCK.

I wonder if the ingenious gentleman that first hit upon digging, tried it with as pleasant a broiling sun over his head as we have. By my soul! if he went to work with his jacket on, it would have warm'd it pretty decently.

VIROLET.

We are slaves, Kilmallock, and must submit. But we are soldiers of Spain—Christian soldiers—

both our faith and our profession, when **Providence**
inflicts calamity, preach patience to us. Murmurs
are fruitless, brother soldier. The fickle goddess,
Fortune, hears not the complainings of the grief-
worn captive.

KILMALLOCK.

Truly now, Count Virolet, I always under-
stood the good lady was blind, but I was never
before told she was dunny. Faith, and that I take
to be the reason she has never been good-natured
enough to listen, when I have reminded her what
a dirty devil she has been to me. First, I was toss'd
out of Tipperary into Spain—where I have fought
these seven years under Ferdinand the Fifth, king
of Castile and Arragon—'till the thumps bestowed
upon me by his Catholic Majesty's enemies, and
be hanged to 'em! have belaboured me up to the
rank of a Captain.

VIROLET.

Right:—of Calatrava; of which gallant order
I boast myself a member.

KILMALLOCK.

Faith, and you may boast—for my own part,
I never had the knack of it. But I have had the
honour, Signior, of fighting side by side with you,
against the Moors of Granada, here.

VIROLET.

And bravely too, good comrade.

KILMALLOCK.

All's one for that.—Well, now I have the honour of being lock'd up with you, in the garden
of an ould whisker-faced Arabian. We have been
prisoners these three months. And here are a
pretty

pretty pair of famous knights, that boaſt them-
ſelves of the gallant Order of Calatrava, with a
bit of a ſhovel popt into their noble hands, digging
away like two planters of potatoes.

VIROLET.

Yet comfort thee, Kilmallock. Granada is cloſe
beſieged. Our royal maſter, Ferdinand, has raiſed
and fortified a town near to their walls. His of-
ficers of moſt approved prowels and expert com-
mand. His men (as report gives out), ſome fifty
thouſand ſtrong; the flower of Caſtile and fair
Arragon.
'Tis, as I hear, a well-ſtock'd hive of war,
Teeming with cloſe compacted swarms of ſol-
    diery;
Who will ſo buzz about their Moorſhips' ears,
Yea, and ſo ſting theſe thin-ſkinn'd Muſſelmen,
That they will ſmart to death with't. Noble
    comrade,
Prove but their arms ſucceſsful, and 'twill cut
A road to freedom for us. Yet that's doubtful—
There were, indeed, a ſhorter way. *(muſing.)*

KILMALLOCK.

Och, then let us be after trudging that. If there
are two roads, Signior, out of captivity, I am always for travelling the ſhorteſt cut, becauſe it bids
fair to be the neareſt.

VIROLET.

Come, I will truſt thee. I do know thee brave;
And in the breaſt where fire-eyed Courage rears
Her rugged throne, ſure honour muſt inhabit.
Yet, dare I truſt thee? *(wavering.)*

KILMALLOCK.

Dare you? Look you, Count Virolet! you dare

do much!—for you are the firſt that ever dare tell me, to my teeth, he held my honour in doubt. Och, fire and oons, and Saint Dominick, to boot! Hark ye, Sir Don! I never was a hunter after other people's ſecrets, as I am not over-fond of keeping what doesn't belong to me. But I am an Iriſhman, mark you me; born a ſubject of his Engliſh Majeſty—Heaven proſper the kings and the country, to the end of time!—and if any Spaniard, Frenchman, or elſe, dare trench upon our honour, by my ſoul we'll fillip them ſoundly, for venturing to call it in queſtion.

VIROLET.

Friend, were the merits of thy nation ſcann'd
From one particular, and thou the ſample,
I ſhould affirm thy countrymen all heart:——
Stuff'd with ſuch various, manly qualities,
That it doth grievouſly perplex their heads
To find fit ſeaſons when to exerciſe them.
He who doth take offence, before 'tis meant,
Is, in himſelf, offending.—Sir, it dwelt not
Within my thought to anger you,

KILMALLOCK.

It did not.—Give me a ſhake of your Spaniſh hand, Signior. I entreat your pardon. Beſhrew me, Count, I am as far from giving an inſult wrongfully, as I am from taking one. And, if I am the ſample you talk of, mark down this for my countrymen, if it pleaſe you.—If my head miſchances to run itſelf, in the dark, againſt the feelings of another, my heart bids me go through fire and water for his ſervice, by way of reparation.

VIROLET.

The ſpirit of thy warm and kindly nature
                                    Shines

Shines thro' thy speech, rough soldier. Hear me,
    comrade!
Thou know'st the governor—

KILMALLOCK.

What, the Moor,—Bulcazin Muley, our master, as he calls himself?—as arrant an ould—

VIROLET.

Your patience. This same Moor, who holds us
    captives,
Has one fair daughter:—beauty's paragon!
Each evening, as the sun begins to sink
Behind the mountain's top, in yonder tower
She'll sit, and, in a simple Moorish ditty,
Pour forth a strain of native melody,
That doth enchant the ravish'd hearer's soul;—
Outwarbling Philomel!

KILMALLOCK.

And, certain, an afternoon's song is a mighty pretty refreshment for a gentleman who has been turning up the mould for eight hours together. But for the life of me now, I cannot guess how it will give him strength to squeeze through the fortifications of Granada.

VIROLET.

Yet, 'tis e'en so, Kilmallock; ~~for this chaunt Is but the burden of our true love's ballad.~~
Briefly, to sweet Zorayda am I sworn;
And she, fair saint, to me.—Some two months
    back,
Worn with fatigue, and leaning on my spade,
In pensive sort, under the cork tree's boughs,
That wave beneath the sullen turret's window,
A female hand, stretch'd thro' the lattice work,
                                              Let

Let fall a letter to me. Thus it ran.
" I am at heart a Christian:—from the slaves,
" You have I singled out:—bear me from hence,
" And fortune, and Zorayda, are yours."

KILMALLOCK.

Och! the creature!

VIROLET.

Oft to her window have I stole at dusk;
When from the tower a silken cord has dropt,
And thus, in mute exchange, we have convey'd
Our written vows;—for speech were dangerous.
Her father (chief about the Moorish king),
Holds the town's key in charge.

KILMALLOCK.

The keys!

VIROLET.

Aye, comrade.—
Our projects ripen. She has will'd me bring
A chosen friend, to back my enterprise;——
And thou art he whom I select, Kilmallock.

KILMALLOCK.

Faith, Count Virolet, and you have chosen as handsomely as heart could desire. For the service of a fair lady, or a small matter of fighting, you may search the world over before you find any better prepared than an Irishman.

VIROLET.

Day wears apace; and the cool evening breeze
Blows fresh and sweetly. *(Zorayda is heard from
    the window)*
Listen!

Song.

Song, ZORAYDA.

    Bewailing! Bewailing!
She sunk, heart broken, on her pillow!
    Her true love's gone,
    Cold, cold as stone:—
Poor Orra now must wear the willow.
    Bewailing! all the night bewailing!
      He lies in gore;
      Her love's no more:—
    Poor Orra's tears are unavailing!

KILMALLOCK.

Och, blessings on her pretty little Moorish throat!—She warbles, for all the world, as natural as a Christian.

(A hand from the tower waves to Virolet).

VIROLET.

Soft.—See, she waves me tow'rd the castle.—
    Comrade,
Tarry, I prithee, near this spot awhile.
I'll cross the moat, and at the eastern gate
Try for admission.—I had near forgot—
Should Sadi pass along—the dapper Moor,
Who guards the slaves, and parcels out our labour,
Draw him aside. Zorayda's entreaty,
And love the patch doth bear a female slave,
Have won him to us. Should he play the churl,
As he is wont, then be this ring thy token,
And he will soften straight. Comrade, farewell!
Now fortune be my speed!
    R.U.E. [*Exit, over the draw-bridge.*

KILMALLOCK.

What a recreation it is to be in love! It sets the heart aching, so delicately, there's no taking
                                      a wink

a wink of sleep for the pleasure of the pain. Cupid, as the poets feign, is stone blind: troth, and they feign very truly:—Or this lady Moor (no disparagement to the Count), had never cast her eyes of affection on a Spaniard; and let a gentleman of Tipperary stand by, without bestowing a glance on him. Yonder trots Sadi, head shepherd over the flock of slaves;—'tis near sun-set, and he comes to pen us all up in the man-fold! *[Retires R.]*

(Enter SADI, *followed by Yusef and Selim).*

SADI.

Out on't! I am sun-roasted, like an over-ripe fig, till I am ready to drop. It looks well now, that I drudge, and you stand idle. Are not you two placed under me, you lop-ear'd knaves you?

Selim.

We are, good Sadi.

SADI.

O cry you mercy.—It seem'd you had forgot the rule of office in all well-govern'd states.

Yusef.

What is it, Sadi?

SADI.

What is it, Sadi? marry, this it is sirrah! and see you note it. When large pay is given for high employment, 'tis the head man's care to take the money, and the deputy's to do the work. Therefore, shew vigilance in your humble departments of labour;—as I, like my brother great men, give example of regularity in my more lofty task of receiving the profits. Remember, 'tis

7. Sad-heard L.

'tis the order of our master, Bulcazin Mulcy, that ye look narrowly to the slaves.

Selim.

I did ne'er relax; I hold the Christians in mortal hate: 'tis meat and drink to me to scourge them.

SADI.

Thou hast indeed, friend, a tolerable twist that way. Thy mind is of the true Mahomet kidney, with the right savage maw of a Musselman. No one can lay to thy charge the guilt of humanity. —Go to—I have noted the diligence of your cruelty; and it shall go hard but I will so order it that, ere long, your deserts shall be showered upon you in plentiful thickness.

Selim.

I thank thee, Sadi. I shall look for thy remembrance.

SADI.

Content thee friend. Thou shalt shortly carry the marks on't.—How now, Christian.—*(to Kilmallock.) who advances.*

KILMALLOCK.

How now, Moor!

SADI.

You must away with me—The sun is near abed.

KILMALLOCK.

Faith, then, Master Sadi, I shall e'en walk this garden, a small half hour, 'till he puts out his candle.

SADI.

SADI.

Were I to chufe now, I would deal with a dozen bluftering captives, rather than one Irifh or Englifh. There is, as it were, a fort of a native kind of a fteady, cool, method of freedom, about thefe Iflanders (as if it grew to them), that keeps its dignity better than any other nation of Chriftendom. Come on, Sir,—you muft forward. *(urging him on)*.

KILMALLOCK.

Mark you, me, Mr. Sadi, the Moor—but you muft ferve me—So you are fafe. Indeed, when a man's in captivity, and would feek favour of a rogue, who has two more at his back, I don't hold it altogether wife to thump him into a kindnefs:—fo, as I would be private here,—here are a couple of doubloons (faved from the old plunderer, your mafter), to leave me to my meditations.

SADI.

Why look ye, Chriftian—It pleafed Mahomet, and my father, when they made me, to make me a Moor—my mother was an humble vaffal here, coop'd up for life, like an old hen, in the caftle; and they found me one morning, hatch'd in Bulcazin's houfe, a new bit of his live property. I was brought up from the fhell, to the bufinefs I am put upon. It may not, haply, hit my humour to crow over the captives:—but if ever I take wing, and fly from the ground of my duty, truft me, Chriftian, I fha'n't be tempted to it with the fcanty grains thrown in my way by the neceffities of the unfortunate. Put up your money Chriftian.

KILMALLOCK.

Faith, and I will.—This is the beft Bantam of the

Kilmallock & L.

the whole black brood of Granada! and I would that every gentleman of England difcharged his truſt with as much honeſty and feeling as my friend here of the copper complexion. You will confent, then, honeſt fellow, to my taking a folitary trot here, without remuneration.

SADI.

I dare not. My maſter is fevere—his fervants pregnant with jealoufy, and fufpicion. Each is even a fpy upon his fellow. Were I found negligent, upon fo flight a ground too, I could not anſwer it, 'twere danger of my place, my life, my— *(Kilmallock ſhews the ring),* eh— umph—oh— hum!——ſtand back you knaves or—— Zorayda! *(whiſpering.)*

KILMALLOCK.

Count Virolet—on to the caftle. *(whiſpering.)*

SADI.

Fellows, this fool's refractory—I'll along with him to our maſter at the caftle—Follow but to the next turning—then leave me, rogues—I'll manage him from thence, I warrant.—Why, how now, Sirrah.—Face to the moat, you rogue —Oh, what you come about friend, do you—On, ſlave, on! [*Exeunt.* *(Sadi driving Kilmallock acrofs the draw-bridge, to the caftle.*

SCENE II. *An apartment in the Caſtle of* Bulcazin Muley.

Enter Bulcazin Muley, *and* Ganem.

BULCAZIN.

So great the Spaniard's army, fay you? Why, By

By Allah, Ganem, 'tis not credible.
It is a Christian fiction: I've no faith in't:—
I have no faith in any thing that's Christian:—
It cannot be.

GANEM.

It is most certain, Sir.
Our spy is new return'd who took their number.
Last night, with 'vantage of the cooling breeze,
That stilly fann'd the parch'd, and sun-crack'd earth,
King Ferdinand (before his new-built town,
That braves our walls), in person did review
Full fifty thousand Spanish men in arms.—
Lusty and fresh:—their polish'd coats of mail
Gleam'd, in faint pride, beneath the silver moon;
Which hung, in maiden sorrow, o'er their heads,
As looking pale at man, intent on slaughter.

BULCAZIN.

Now may the pestilent dew of vaporous night
Pierce to their marrow!—Sap their hated bones!
The flagging air blow hot and moist upon them!
May the high Prophet, who protects our battles,
Pour, from the ponderous, and scowling clouds,
Deluge on deluge down! till the swoll'n Darro
O'erflood its limits; and the sodden Christians
Rot, like starv'd carrion, in the drowned field.
What, has the King sent for me?

GANEM.

Even now.—
He waits your coming, Sir, at the Alhambra.

BULCAZIN.

Say I attend his bidding.—Stay; come back.—
Evermore to and fro! ever more care!
Council, despatches, court, mosque, garrison!
Threading the city's avenues, to goad

The

The sluggish guard to duty;—then at night,
Eves-dropping to entrap the mutineer;
Or plodding by the blue and paly lamp
In painful rumination. This it is
To be a governor!—A dogged mule,
That climbs the craggy mountain with his load,
Enjoys a life of ease to't. I do envy
The vilest beast, that sweats beneath his burthen;
For mine's upon the brain. Dull, thoughtless
    hound!
Why art not gone?

            GANEM.

  It was your will, so please you,
To call me back again.

           BULCAZIN.

  O, true, good Ganem!
Go to Zorayda, my daughter;—tell her
Ere I go forth, I fain would speak with her.
                          [*Exit Ganem.*
There is another toil!—to guard a daughter!
And watch the youthful shoots of disposition,
In a green growing girl.
She has seem'd sad of late; but yesternoon,
As I did question her, in casual talk,
When she had been at mosque, a stealing tear
Dropt from her cheek, upon my hand.—At
    mosque!
The silly fool is vapourish.—her mother,
That's dead, was Christian—umph!—Oh, Ma-
    homet!
If that I thought 'twere so, my scymetar
Should—pish! it cannot be. Sweet wench, I
    wrong her.

                               Enter

R. — Enter ZORAYDA.

ZORAYDA.

I am here, father; would you aught with me?

BULCAZIN.

Come hither, wench.—I muſt to the Alhambra.
Should Giaffer arrive ere my return,
There is a writing, ſeal'd up in my cabinet,
(This is the key), you muſt deliver to him.
Why doſt not take it, dreamer? My Zorayda!
Art thou not well? my child! why doſt thou tremble?

ZORAYDA.

'Tis that your ſternneſs terrifies me, father.
My heart's brimfull, when you are kind to me—
And my eyes too:—no wonder, then, I tremble
When you ſpeak angerly.

BULCAZIN.

My dear, dear daughter!
Cheer thee, my child! The duties, which of late,
Do throng upon me, may go nigh, belike,
To make me ſomewhat fretful. Theſe vile Chriſtians
Vex thy poor father, ſore, Zorayda.
Would it not glad thee, wench, to ſee theſe dogs
Dragg'd through our town in chains?

ZORAYDA.

No, truſt me, father:
For when the captives paſs, that dig our garden,
Pining in wretchedneſs, and ſpirit-broken,
Poor hearts! I turn my head aſide, and weep,
To ſee a ſight ſo piteous. Surely, father,
When heaven made Man, it never was ordain'd

That

$\overline{\underline{17.}}$

R.- Agnes.

That he should make his fellow-creatures
    slaves,
And gall them with such cruelty.

BULCAZIN.

   How now!
Dost lean to them? Observe me well, Zorayda—
I do misdoubt thee heavily; yea, heavily.
These Christians, on whose miseries your eye,
Lavish in baby bounty, drops a tear,
Have been our nation's scourge. This wretched
    corner,
This Moorish kingdom of Granada, here,
(A very patch on Spain's broad territory,
Which all was our's), is all that they have left us;
Therefore take heed. I could more readily
Suck poison from a cold and speckled toad,
And, as I drain'd his venom, think the bees
Distill'd their mountain-honey on my lip,
Than smother in my breast that rooted hate
I bear a loathsome Christian. Mark me, girl!
Thou art my heart's dear love: Do not prove
    changeling:
Should'st mingle with my heart's antipathy,
Unmov'd, I'd see thee drooping on a death-bed,
And let my curse fall bitter on thee. Think on't;
And so farewell! [*Exit L.*

ZORAYDA.

  —Alas, the day, my father!
Could'st use thy daughter thus! and stab thine
    enemies
Through thy poor child! Those enemies could
    teach thee
A heaven-born duty in their holy writ,
(Unpractis'd here), called Christian charity,
Worth all the Koran. How now, Agnes!

Enter

Enter AGNES.

AGNES.

Haste you, madam!—Count Virolet is uneas[y]
at your stay.—He is stalking to and fro you[r]
chamber, to give his patience exercise.

ZORAYDA.

Softly, beseech you! Why he knew my fathe[r]
(Who is but now gone forth to the Alhambra)
Sent for me on the sudden. Tell me, Agnes,
Are Christian lovers ever thus impetuous?
Trust me, I fear them rash, and sudden, Agnes.
Will they not tarry?

AGNES.

Truly, Madam, I am little skill'd in 'em, I! m[y]
father kept me close at home, in Andalusia, till [I]
should go as a lay-sister to the Ursulines; and
on that day, as we journey'd thither, the Moors
as you know, Madam, pursued my poor father
and made me a slave.—None have discoursed t[o]
me tenderly, but Sadi. I have seen little of Christia[n]
love;—but I have often heard say 'tis not of th[e]
waiting sort. Will it please you go, Madam?

ZORAYDA.

Ay, wench, and further too than it may pleas[e]
me.
Girl, here has been my father, loud in anger:—
He has so wrung me, with unkindly words!
And all about these Christians. Wer't thou me[,]
What course would'st thou follow, Agnes?

AGNES.

I have but a shallow wit to advise, Madam;—
bu[t]

H. M. B.

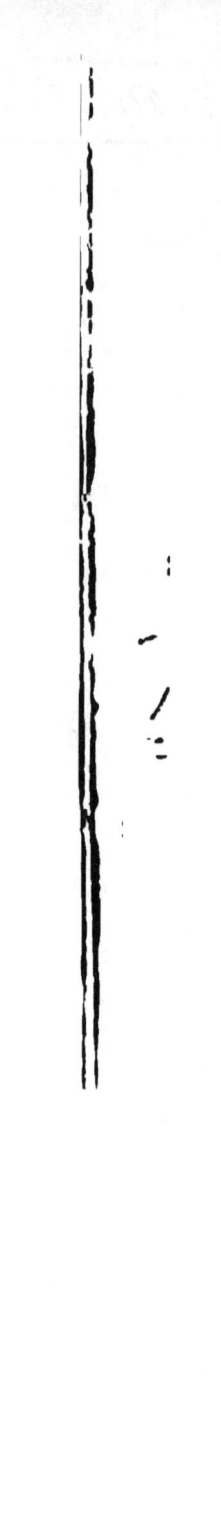

but I would, for my own part, do like other Spanish girls, when they have opportunity.

ZORAYDA.
And what do they when fathers are unkind?

AGNES.
They run away, Madam.

ZORAYDA.
Beshrew me, now, my heart does sink within me—
Yet I can ne'er forget my mother's council,
As I watch'd by her on the night she died.
And there is something here that whispers me
I shall not be at peace till I am Christian.
Should Virolet's entreaty, and the harshness
I meet with here, at home, hasten my flight,
Would'st follow with me, Agnes?

AGNES.
Follow you! O, the virgin! It shews little love to follow you into liberty—Would I had the means to shew more!

ZORAYDA.
Wherefore, good Agnes?

AGNES.
Because you have been kind to me. I was brought here a slave; torn from my poor old father. My heart had broke with sorrow but for you, Lady. You took me to you, and dried the tears, that ran trickling down my face, with words of comfort and compassion. My fortunes have been always humble, Lady; but I can be grateful and trusty; and I should be weary of

my

my life if I forgot to love those whose charity and
goodness had preserved it. I would follow you
through the world, Lady.

ZORAYDA.

Sweet heart, I thank thee! listen to me, Agnes:
My father will return anon; meanwhile
(A chance which never may befall again),
I have his cabinet in charge—he keeps
The key in't of the little western gate,
Through which, in private, he is wont to pass
Forth from the city. Virolet has moved me
With reasons strong, and honey-sweet persuasion.
If zeal and earnest movements of the soul,
Which bid me shun the path of unbelievers,
May plead a maid's excuse, for leaping, thus,
Beyond the pale of seeming, surely, Agnes,
I may be bold to venture. O, my father!
We must away to night.

AGNES.

To night, Lady!

ZORAYDA.

Or never, girl.

AGNES.

What—and unprotected, Madam.

ZORAYDA.

No Agnes; Violet will guard us.

AGNES.

True, Madam; yet he is but one—and in the
night,

night, Madam, I am apt to feel difheartened. I could wifh now—

ZORAYDA.

What, girl?

AGNES.

Why, of a truth, then, Madam, if Sadi went with us, methinks I fhould feel more valiant.

ZORAYDA.

Take heed, good Agnes;—fearch thy bofom well;
Nor draw this half-converted Moor along,
To fwell thy giddy pride, and woman's lightnefs.
My purpofes are pure and folemn, Agnes:—
Did not a holy light direct my courfe,
Not all the love which I do bear to Virolet
Could tear me from a father:—therefore, Agnes,
Probe to thy heart; if thou doft find it fteady
Unto this Moor, bring him away with thee;
Elfe fully not my facred enterprife,
With ill-befeeming levity. Anon,
Thoul't find me in my chamber. [*Exit R*

AGNES.

What a world of pains it faves to have one's mind ready made up to be married at fhort notice! I had loft, elfe, the time for my journey, in debating on the fitnefs of my company. Heigho! I would my Sadi were a fhade lighter. No flave-driver in all Granada has a fweeter difpofition. Father Sebaftian, a captive here, good foul! fays, that when a Moor turns Chriftian, faith will work any thing—I wonder if it ever whitens the fkin.—'Bating his complexion, Sadi,

Sadi, is a proper man, with the beſt curl'd hair of any in Spain.—Would the evening muſter were over, and the guard placed for the night!

SONG.

When the hollow drum has beat to bed;
When the little fifer hangs his head;
  Still and mute,
  The Mooriſh flute,
And nodding guards watch wearily;
  Then will we,
  From priſon free,
March out by moon-light, cheerily.

When the Mooriſh cymbals claſh by day,
When the brazen trumpets ſhrilly bray,
  The ſlave, in vain,
  May then complain,
Of tyranny and knavery.
  Would he know,
  His time to go,
And ſlyly ſlip from ſlavery——

'Tis when the hollow drum has beat to bed;
When the little fifer hangs his head;
  Still and mute,
  The Mooriſh flute,
And nodding guards watch wearily;
  Oh then muſt he,
  From priſon free,
March out by moon-light, cheerily!

[Going R.

L.—Enter SADI.

SADI.

Hiſt! hiſt! Agnes!—whither away!

         AGNES.

AGNES.

Sadi.—I was going to the lady Zorayda. Thou art come to my very wiſh.

SADI.

To ſee what luck is!—That the appearance of a man-Moor ſhould tickle thus the inclinations of a little ſhe-Chriſtian?—Did'ſt really wiſh to ſee me, Agnes?

AGNES.

You have been always welcome to me, Sadi;— ever ſince you brought me the little purſe of piaſtres, to ſend to my father, who is in want. Though the lady Zorayda's bounty prevented my taking it, I love thee for thy heart, dearly, Sadi.

SADI.

I doubt now, whether that be not the beſt thing about a man that a wench can take a fancy to, after all. Should a knave, that could be flinty-hearted to a poor girl in diſtreſs, fall in my way, and pro- poſe to chop natures with me, I would not change with him, tho' his face were as white as a cauli- flower. Kiſs me, Agnes: *(kiſſes her.)*—'Tis thus I have been converted.

AGNES.

Nay, now.

SADI.

By the Maſs 'tis true. Had forty fat monks fail'd in preaching Mahomet out of me, thy lips, Agnes, would convince me.

AGNES.

Pr'ythee liſten—the lady Zorayda will away to-night.

SADI.

SADI.

I guefs'd as much.

AGNES.

Aye, marry, why fo?

SADI.

There is a captive waits now for Count Violet—his fworn friend—who is to be partner in the flight. He feems well fitted for danger and fecrecy. He is both brawney and faithful. I had brought him hither, but I was told you were here, Agnes.

AGNES.

Well, Sadi, thou know'ft I am trufted with all.

SADI.

True:—but to be plain, he is of the Irifh nation; and when a man would talk bufinefs with a female, thofe of his country are noted for taking off her attention.

AGNES.

Out on thee! thou would'ft turn jealous fhortly. Well, night is near; and when I am away with the lady Zorayda, thou wilt think kinder of me.

SADI.

How!—what!—what doft thou go with her, Agnes?

AGNES.

Surely.

SADI.

What, and leave——umph!

AGNES.

AGNES.

Would'st have me tarry behind when my good lady is in danger, and lofe too the means of freedom? Thou know'st that—why what is it ails thee, Sadi?—art not well?

SADI.

Yes—nothing—'tis a—'tis the cholic, Agnes. To-night, faid you?

AGNES.

Aye, Sadi:—and here—I have a little rofary; you fhall keep it for my fake: let me tie it on thy neck—So—thou'lt think of me now fometimes, when thou look'ft at it, Sadi?

SADI.

Agnes, I—I cannot well fpeak at prefent. I thought we had bid fair to ftick together thro' life. I will not upbraid you. Alla blefs you, Agnes! and fhould you meet a lighter-fkin'd lover, may he be as fond and as faithful as the poor dufky fellow you leave broken-hearted behind you!

AGNES.

Nay, but Sadi—

SADI.

Farewell! I look'd fhortly to have been taken to be chriften'd, had you prov'd fteady to me. I am now, neither Moor nor Catholic:—and fhould thy unkindnefs wear me to the grave, I can claim little better than pye-bald burial. Go, Agnes, and happinefs be with you!

AGNES.

AGNES.

And when I go a ſtep without you, Sadi, may I never know what 'tis to be happy again.

SADI.

Eh!—

AGNES.

O, my poor, dear Sadi!—forgive the pain I have put thee to; but you ſeem'ſt jealous of me, Sadi; and in puniſhing you for't, beſhrew me, now, but I have puniſh'd myſelf.

SADI.

Now could I be difpleas'd in my turn, were I not too glad to be angry. Your hand, Agnes.—I have offended, and thou carry'ſt the whip. Do not fear finding me guilty again; for thou haſt, now, laid it on ſo tightly, that were I to live a thouſand years, the ſmart on't would never out of my memory.

AGNES.

Comfort thee, Sadi. The lady Zorayda has confented that thou ſhould'ſt along with me. Liberty is now before me, and as thou loveſt me, let us away. Prepare thee quickly, for night is coming on.

SADI.

Farewell, maſter! I will pack up ſtrait. With five years pay, a true heart, three ſhirts, Chriſtianity in my head, and thee under my arm, will I, this night, take a long leave of Granada. Hang care, and a guittar at thy back, Agnes, and we'll jog merrily over the mountains into Andaluſia.

DUETT.

Ready at the Lumps.

DUETT.

Sadi *and* Agnes.

SADI.

O! happy tawney moor!—when you, love,
Climb the mountain with your true love,
    Will you, by the way,
    The music play?
Your sweet guittar a tinkling, Sadi
Listens to his Spanish lady.
        Tang, tanki, tanki, tang, tang,
        Tanki, tanki, tay.

AGNES.

O! bonny tawney moor! together,
As we brave the wind and weather,
    Won't you, by the way,
    From Agnes stray?
While their guittars are tinkling, Sadi,
Love no other Spanish lady.
        Tang, tanki, tanki, tang, tang,
        Tanki, tanki, tay.

SADI.

Cease, pretty Agnes, cease;—no beauty
E'er could draw me from my duty.
    Let them, all the day,
    Their music play.

AGNES.

Then my guittar a tinkling, Sadi,
Follow now your Spanish lady.
        Tang, tanki, tanki, tang, tang,
        Tanki, tanki, tay.

BOTH.

26   THE MOUNTAINEERS.

BOTH.

AGNES. ⎧ 'Then my guittar, &c.
SADI. ⎨ Her sweet guittar a tinkling, Sadi
       ⎩ Follows now his Spanish lady.
　　　　Tang, tanki, tanki, tang, tang
　　　　　Tanki, tanki, tay.
　　　　　　　　R. [*Exeunt*

✢ The Stage a little darkened.

SCENE III. *The Bavarambla (or market place) in the town of* Granada.
From R. through Archway.
Enter the Moorish guard, Officers, &c. with standard and pikes. *March to the front of the Stage, and form a Crescent.*

PACHA.

Ali Beg!

ALI.

Here, my Pacha. *Pacha.*

Ali, having, this day, raised thee from the ranks, 'tis fit I do commend the care with which thou hast drawn forth the soldiery. How long hast thou borne arms, Ali?

ALI.

Five and twenty years, so please you, the last moon of Moharram.

PACHA.

And see, thou art now promoted. Mark, Ali, the advantage of the Muffelman army. While the worn-out Catholick soldier retires, that a younger man may fill his place, then is the happy moor
　　　　　　　　　　　　advanced

advanced to all the glorious fatigues of duty. His aching bones never draw upon him the neglect of his officer;—who heaps threefold employment upon his aged shoulders, in reward of his paft service!—Thou haft now, Ali, the full pay of thy deceafed predeceffor.

ALI.

Thy flave thanks thee, noble Pacha!

PACHA.

Out of which, Ali, thou haft, fimply, to maintain his four widows, left behind him.—Blefs thyfelf, Ali, that thou art born to fight under Moorifh leaders;—who are diftinguifhed by fuch charity as is never thought of in a Chriftian army. Is each man here according to the roll?

ALI

All.

PACHA.

I will firft addrefs them:—then, Ali, march them to their pofts for the night.—Moors and foldiers! under the renown'd Mahomet, Boabdili, Chiquito, King of Granada! 'Tis the regard of your commander now cautions you that you relax not from your charge. My tendernefs bids you be vigilant, through the night; that ye may 'fcape the bow-ftring to which I fhould, otherwife, fentence you, in the morning- The true foldier thinks his duty a pleafure; and none of you, my honeft fellows, on pain of death, fhall forego the pleafure of your duty. The Spaniards, who befiege us, are Chriftians. You are Moors. Remember, then, you fight in the caufe of your Religion:—maintain its amiable doctrines to the laft, and fhew your enemies no mercy!—Now to your watch

watch:—Where, out of kindnefs, I forbid you to fortify your ftomachs againft the raw air of the night;—for he who lifts wine to his mouth, my worthy friends, fpeedily lofes his head.—Strike and away.

Grand Chorus of Moorifh Soldiers.

The fun is funk:—and, from afar,
See the pale bright evening ftar!
Soon the wolf begins to prowl;
Soon the fhrilly fcreeching owl
Through the air her death wing claps,
And at the fick man's window flaps;
While, on the rampart ftrong and fteep,
Their filent watch the Centries keep.
Hark to the heavy rolling drum!
The hour of nightly duty's come.
Lufty Moors! Obey command!
March to your pofts, and take your ftand!
    March!   [*Exeunt.*

END OF ACT I.

ACT

Piccola. Ibi.
Cimbali. Drum

~~Henry~~
1. 2. Mnl. Hark ye, Lobo Jocho, mine host.
Jocho. What say you Señor?

ACT. II.

SCENE I. *The inside of a Venta (or Spanish Inn), in Andalusia.*

A Stable door in the back Scene—over it a hayloft. A lamp against the wall. A fire in the midst of the room. Muleteers discovered, drinking.

Enter Lope Tocho (the Host).

TOCHO.

Bravely pull'd, gallants! and merrily! Of all the worthy tuggers at a bottle, give me your noble Gentlemen carriers!—who while away the heavy hours in the amusing exercise of driving mules over the mountains.

1st. MULETEER.

Certain, mine host, in respect to deep drinking, we muleteers have hard heads.

TOCHO.

Nay, that ye have. Ye are a pack of the hardest heads of any in Spain. Fifteen years have I been host of this Venta, at the foot of the Sierra de Ronda. Tocho is my name. Lope Tocho, of the province of Andaulusia. I live by the hunger and thirst of the traveller;—and keep a yearly account of my thanks due to stomachs and throats:—and in striking my balance, Gentlemen, I find the generous maw of a Gentleman muleteer,

calls

calls for five times the food of the best grandee's
that journeys the country.—Worthy Signiors! I
am your sweet throats, and stomachs, debtor and
servant. *(drinks.)*

2d. MULETEER.

Methinks, ~~mine host~~, the kid you gave us at
supper, had somewhat of an unsavory smell with
it. It did, as it were, stink most abominably.

TOCHO.

I know not well how that could be, Signior!
for I have bestowed wonderous pains on it, these
three weeks past, to keep it sweet. For delicate
eating, and right Malaga, there is not an Inn can
match me between this and Antequera—~~No,
verily, not one.~~

3d. MULETEER.

'Tis a wild road thither.

TOCHO.

You will not set eyes on a house till you reach
the town, Signior. 'Tis some league and a half,
over the mountains;—and affords, truly, but indifferent
accommodation. Here's to your good entertainment
on the way, Signiors. *(drinks.)*

1st. MULETEER.

Hast any news stirring in these parts, honest
Lope?

TOCHO.

War, Gentlemen—War, with the Moors— we
are here on the skirts of their kingdom of
Granada—and in the very heart of those skirts, as
I may say, King Ferdinand of Castile and Arragon,
does now most closely stick. Saint Jago be his
speed,

speed, say I! I could never away with these infidels. Their's must needs be a devil of a religion that forbids the drinking of wine.

2d. MULETEER.
One cup to the Christian cause, mine host!

TOCHO.
Right willingly—Confusion to the barbarous Moors!—and may the King of a Christian people never want loving subjects to drink his prosperity, and give the enemies of humanity a drubbing! *(all drink.)*

4th. MULETEER.
I pri'thee Perez, as we pass'd through Cordova, dids't bethink thee to get my pack saddle mended for the blind mule?

3d. MULETEER.
Truly, brother, I cared not to pay five good reals, when I may never chance to see them again.

4th. MULETEER. *(starting up.)*
Santa Maria! Reflect on the honour of a Spaniard! Death and my mustachios! Thou shalt not live. *(draws his stilletto.)*

TOCHO *(interposing).*
Nay Gentlemen!—Here's goodly work! Sweet Signior of the mules! you mistake him. Honour is a delicate matter—he could not mean it. Noble driver of the beasts, be pacified.

4th. MULETEER.
Wound my integrity! 'tis dearer to a Spaniard than life. 'Tis an affront cannot be mended.

TOCHO.

TOCHO.

It shall, honourable Signior! and your pack-saddle too.——Good friend, throw the cold water of your repentance on the fire of his anger. Come, 'twas a hasty speech: say so, and be friends.

3d. MULETEER.

Well I——I meant not to wound his honour.

TOCHO.

See there, now!

4th. MULETEER.

I—I am content:——But remember, in future, brother, what is due to a Spaniard. Insult him, and he will compass the globe for revenge. Your hand: my honour is satisfied: we will clean our mules together, in fellowship, as usual.

TOCHO.

By our Lady, 'tis sensibly said! many a noble life has been lost, on a point of honour—no more difficult to be settled than this! Another cup to drown animosity.

1st. MULETEER.

Content: and then to rest. 'Tis deep midnight, and we must rise betimes, on our way to Ubeda.

TOCHO.

Mass, you muleteers, in the way of pleasant travelling, have a wearisome life of it.

1st. MULETEER.

The grandee, mine host, that sleeps upon down, dreams little of our hardships. Yet we can be
merry

merry, too. Let us troll a round, and, then, go stretch on the straw.

GLEE.

MULETEERS.

You high born Spanish noblemen, you dons, and
    cavaliers!
Ah! little do you think upon the lowly Mule-
    teers!
To earn an honest livelihood, what toils, what
    cares, we know,
      Small our gain, great our pain,
      O'er the hill, o'er the plain,
      Parch'd with heat, drench'd with rain,
      Still the Muleteer must go!

When darkness overtakes us, our mules to
    droop begin;
Fatigued and spent, what joy we feel to reach
    the wish'd-for inn!
We drain the wine cag jollily, we tofs it to and
    fro:—
      While to sleep as we creep,
      Maritornes may weep,
      That, when daylight does peep,
      Then the Muleteer must go.

(A knocking at the door of the Venta.—A voice calls without, "Soho! within there ho!").

TOCHO.

Travellers, by faint Dominick!—and, by the noise, of authority, Perequillo! *(knocking again)* 'tis ever thus.—I never knew your great man on the wrong side of the House that ceased his clamour till he got in!

R.-*Enter* PEREQUILLO.

Perequillo, look to the gate. Signiors, a good rest. That way to your straw-chamber gentlemen. *(pointing to the stable-door.)*

1st. MULETEER.

'Tis fit we be called by times, mine host.

TOCHO.

Perequillo, knock at the Gentlemens stable door by day-break.
(Knocking still—Muleteers go into the stable.)
Out, you gaping rogue, run to the gate!

PEREQUILLO.

These travellers rob a good fellow of more sleep than the Musquitos. [*Exit.*

TOCHO.

I fear me, the tough old cock will never crow "day light" again. Six years has he serv'd me for a dial; and now must I twist his neck, to give these gallants a supper. Truth is, we are marveloufly scant of provisions.

Enter FLORANTHE, *dressed as a Cavalier, leaning on* ROQUE.

ROQUE.

So—cheerly I warrant!—Come, a seat, now, quickly. Bestir, bestir!

TOCHO.

Is not his worship well?

ROQUE.

Cannot your worship see?—a chair you—— (*Tocho brings a chair.*) So!

FLORANTHE

FLORANTHE *(sitting down.)*

I faint, almoſt, with wearineſs.

ROQUE.

Plague on your dark nights, and foul ways!—why doſt not mend them?

TOCHO.

Truly, Gentlemen, there be thoſe, in this quarter, that might better the foul ways—but, for mending the dark nights, we are, I do confeſs, ill furniſh'd with work-men.

ROQUE.

Art furniſhed with a good bed, friend?

TOCHO.

The beſt in Spain. We are much, and nobly frequented here, Signior—we have, this night, a company of ſome twenty.

ROQUE.

A murrain light on 'em! then they have occupied the bed-chamber.

TOCHO.

Why, as luck would have it, they repoſe in the ſtable. Each traveller, ſignior, to his fancy.

FLORANTHE.

I would to reſt, friend.—We have journey'd far:
At ſun riſe, we muſt needs ſet forth again.
I am nigh ſinking with fatigue!

ROQUE.

No wonder poor heart!—My mafters nag, friend, is the rougheſt pacing beaſt in Spain. 'Twould tire a devil.

TOCHO.

Would not the Signior Cavalier pleafe to refreſh? I have the remains of a kid that is delicious—and we are noted here for chicken.

FLORANTHE.

Oh, I do loath the very name of food.

TOCHO.

Loath food!—This is a mighty ſimple youth.

FLORANTHE.

Prepare my chamber, friend, and fear not you.
'Though I betake me fupperlefs to bed,
I will content thee (for I know the cuſtom)
As I had banqueted.

TOCHO.

The youth is not altogether fo ſimple as I thought him. Signior Hidalgo, your chamber ſhall be prepared ſtraight. For an excellent ſupper, if you eat it not, 'tis your lofs; which is hard: if you pay for it not, 'tis mine; which is harder—for I am a poor man, ſir, that would willingly grow richer.

ROQUE. (*x 772.*)

Away, you knave! and obey orders: fee to the chamber—look to the horfes, and return, anon, with fome wine: my maſter is faint with travel.

TOCHO.

TOCHO.

I shall, friend. This now must be a delicate bit of smock-fac'd nobility. Should Providence rain beards, 'twould do no harm to his face if his chin were thrust out in the shower. [*Exit.*

FLORANTHE.

Now tell me, Roque,—how far is't to the mountain?

ROQUE.

We are nigh the foot on't, lady—we had founder'd by the way else. Heaven reft those tender joints! for they must needs ache, with jolting thus from Seville. My tough bones, though well seaſon'd in camps and marches, are fairly bump'd into a rheumatism.

FLORANTHE.

I care but little for my aching limbs,
Did not my heart ache with them. The encounter
We look will follow this same pilgrimage
Makes me most sad, and heavy.

ROQUE.

'Tis strange, now, the labour some will undergo to encounter melancholy! and truly, I left Don Octavian in poor plight to amend the spirits of those who wish him well. What between love and loneliness, by living in the woods, he is clean an alter'd man. I once was enamoured of a pin-maker's daughter of Segovia, and found solitude did but encrease my pain;—so I e'en cur'd myself on't, in three weeks, by keeping my mistress company.

FLORANTHE.

FLORANTHE.

Was't in the wild part of the mountain, Roque,
Where late you saw Octavian?

ROQUE.

Good faith, in the very bosom, here, of the Sierra de Ronda. With a full heart, and an empty bottle, was I trudging from Granada to Seville—to bring the sad news of my master, Count Virolet, your ladyship's brother, being taken by the Moors: when in crossing the mountain, here, among other game started by the way, I at last put up a man—(Don Octavian, as your ladyship knows) who sprung from a thicket, and flew from my sight like a wild duck.

FLORANTHE.

Alas, for pity! after twelve long months,
To meet him thus again! Now hear me, Roque—
I think thou art attach'd to all our house;
For I have heard my late lost father say,
Ere thou could'st lisp thy service had begun in't.

ROQUE.

If my mother's word may pass, lady, I held my first birth-day in't, up four pair of stairs, in the right hand garret that looks over the fish-pond: And if ever I prove thankless for being born in the one, I would I might, that moment, be dragg'd thro' the other.

FLORANTHE.

Thou didst first trudge an urchin to the field
With my poor father:—lately thou hast follow'd
My brother Virolet. Though train'd to arms,
And a rough soldier, Roque, I think thou can'st
                                        Extend

Extend thy honeſt love of this our family
E'en to a female of the ſtock.

ROQUE.

A ſoldier, lady, can extend his love to the
female of any family. But to you, Donna Floranthe, daughter of my old maſter, and ſiſter of
my young one!——What would not I give now
to ſee you beſet with a good round dozen of your
enemies!—Well, I am getting in years—but they
ſhould have a taſte of old Roque's ſkill in the
cudgel, yet.

FLORANTHE.

I do believe thee, Roque:—therefore, good
    fellow,
To-morrow, when we ſeek this mountain's gloom,
Searching its caves, and tangled labyrinths,
Where the wolf nightly howls againſt the moon,
And lowleſs Plunder, on his hungry watch,
Lurks, meditating murder—then, good Roque,
Should any ill befal,—and heaven knows
What may befal me!—

ROQUE.

What! Donna Floranthe! and I with you?—
They muſt fight hard, lady, that would harm you.
—An you take the road to dying, Madam, by
your leave, I muſt go foremoſt.

FLORANTHE.

I would not have it ſo, good Roque. Live
    thou,
Whate'er betide, to tell my ſimple ſtory;
Leſt ſlander blot a luckleſs maiden's fame,
And no one left to clear her memory.

ROQUE.

ROQUE.

Truly, Madam, I am the worst teller of a story of any in Spain. I can only say that my old master, your father, bid you love Don Octavian; but as old Gentlemen will sometimes change their minds, he, after a while, charged you to love another— which ill suiting Don Octavian's humour, he fairly ran his rival through the body; fled in despair; and hadn't been heard of for a twelvemonth—'till I started him here in the woods:—when coming to tell you the news, I found my old master, rest his soul! at peace; you single; the wounded man recovered, and married to a rich one-ey'd widow, of Salamanca.

FLOR'ANTHE.

'Twill be a faithful history, old soldier.

ROQUE.

I trust not, Madam: for I shall then proceed to specify that you went forth, in search of your lover, and died by the way; which I hope, saving your presence, will be one of the roundest lies that ever found passage thro' the mouth of a soldier.

Enter LOPE TOCHO—*(with a bottle and glass.)*

FLORANTHE.

Now, friend, hast thou prepar'd my chamber?

TOCHO.

'Twould ha' done your heart good to see the warming-pan slide between the white sheets; you will sleep in air'd snow, Signior. Would it please you take a whet, ere you creep betwixt 'em?

(Offering the wine).

FLORANTHE.

Ready at the Lamps—

FLORANTHE.

Not a drop, hoſt; I will to reſt; and Roque, Get thee to bed. We muſt away at dawn, hoſt. Refreſh thee, Roque—and ſo good night, good fellow. [*Exit R*

TOCHO.

Do you not follow your maſter, to help him undreſs, friend?

ROQUE.

That is *my* buſineſs, friend.

TOCHO.

By our lady, I never found a gentleman know his own buſineſs better, and do it worſe! what may thy maſter be, friend?

ROQUE.

That is *his* buſineſs, friend:—but for me, I am a ſoldier; and have learnt ſomewhat in the wars.

TOCHO.

Aye, marry—I would fain know what 'tis.

ROQUE.

'Tis, when I ſee a knave thruſt his noſe into the buſineſs of another, to tweak it very luſtily.

TOCHO.

Signior, I do reverence a ſoldier—but I never much cared to ſee him go through his manœuvres.

ROQUE.

Follow. I ſhall to the loft, and turn in, an hour or two. Bring the bottle after me, and place it on the hay-truſs, where I lay me down.

[*Exit, up the ladder into the loft.*]

TOCHO.

TOCHO.

And, if I carry my countenance near the finge
and thumb of such a nose-tweaker again, I woul
my face might want a handle ever after. Oons
I shall dream of nothing, all night, but the hug
paw of a trooper.—'I weak! well—let him bu
lye one hour in the loft, and he'll be the best flea
bitten bully in Andalusia. *R.* [*Exi*

SCENE II. *The Sierra de Ronda.*

Enter VIROLET, ZORAYDA, *and* KILMALLOCK

VIROLET.

Love, not a word? Good faith, it is no wonder
Thou must be sadly worn, Zorayda!
Sleep hangs upon those pretty eyes of thine,
And dulls their lustre. Art not wond'rous weary

ZORAYDA.

The Spirit, Christian, that did prompt my flight
Will give me strength, I warrant, to endure it.
'Twere evil in me to forget my father—
But, were he now less heavy on my thoughts,
I should be found a stouter traveller.

KILMALLOCK.

What a sweet little Moor it is!—Och! sh
can never be her father's daughter. By Sain
Dominick, Count, this same escaping from fa
tiguing work is mighty hard labour.

VIROLET.

A few leagues more, and we shall reach th
town

*Lor. I tremble in these wilds
For my dear Agnes!*

That skirts this mountain.—There, to horse again;
And thence to Seville:—to my friends, Zorayda!
Where the strong power of our holy Church
Shall seal my title to the sweetest convert
That ever yet abjured her heresy,
And shelter'd in it's bosom.

ZORAYDA.

Wou'd we were there! for though I have been told
Your duty teaches patience to the sufferer,
I fear this painful march may make me peevish;
And that were sinful. Do not mock me, love;
But I shall prove, I doubt, a sorry Christian.

KILMALLOCK.

Oh, faith, you'll be as good as the best. I never knew a young Christian lady, yet, that was not impatient when she was going to be married.— Well, this mountain is what they call the Sierra de Ronda—close to the borders of Andalusia— here we are in the middle of it—with as fine a prospect of a dark night, as a traveller would wish to look round upon.

VIROLET.

Would our companions were come up! 'tis strange
They loiter thus, ~~Zorayda! I tremble in these wilds, For my poor Agnes~~.

KILMALLOCK.

And that copper devil, Sadi, too! Certain now, our horses founder'd at the foot of the mountain that he might stay behind to look after them:— and the girl sat down, weeping, by his side, to help him.

ZORAYDA.

ZORAYDA.

Poor wench! her heart is ftored with kindnefs

KILMALLOCK.

Och, it's brimful. But this is the firft time I ever heard fquatting down to cry was the way to help a man to pull horfes out of the mire.

VIROLET.

Wilt forward, fweet? or fhall we tarry for them?

ZORAYDA.

Sooth, I am weary now—Yet I could on—
And yet I could not.—Shall I tell thee, love;—
I could not leave this honeft wench behind,
And fleep in quiet. She is humble born;
But truft me, Chriftian, I do fee no caufe
Why I fhould blufh in feeling for the lowly.
The peafant, pining on his bed of ftraw,
Should draw as warm a tear from melting pity,
As when a monarch fuffers.

VIROLET.

Lovely excellence!
Virtue, all fweet before, fteals o'er thy lip
As the foft breeze that bends the modeft rofe,
Grown fweeter in it's paffage. Thou may'ft preach—
When rigid fchoolmen fail, and win with gentlenefs;
Caufe even fhame to fpread the proud man's cheek,
And make the world in love with charity.

(Drum beats at a diftance).

Hark! heard you not a diftant drum, Kilmallock?

KILMALLOCK.

KILMALLOCK.

Faith, and it is a drum! It does a soldier's heart good to hear it thump—though to be sure, now, it is not quite so convenient. These Moors, though they are most of 'em pen'd up in Granada, keep skirmishing, and trotting about all over the province. Friends or enemies, it isn't civil in 'em to keep a clatter at this time o'night, and disturb us lodgers in the mountain.

ZORAYDA.

I sink with terror.

KILMALLOCK.

Nay, that you shall not. It never shall be said, that a woman sunk in the hour of distress while a man stands by that can hold up her chin.

ZORAYDA.

Let us not forward now, beseech you, Virolet;
Trust me, there's danger in't.—Poor Agnes, too!
Seek me some covert in this tufted mountain,
Where, till the day appears, I may repose,
And rest in safety.

VIROLET.

Come, Zorayda!
And the next bank, o'ercanopied with trees,
Must now, perforce, be thy rude lodging, sweet!
I, and my comrade, will watch near thee, cheerly!
So—cheerly!—all will yet be well.
(Exeunt Virolet and Zorayda.)

KILMALLOCK.

I'll hover about here, as an out-post. When a man watches in the dark, by himself, on a mountain,

tain, he's rather apt to be lonefome; but if he chances to be upon duty there, to ferve a friend, and guard female innocence, he needs but call in his own thoughts to be in mighty agreeable company. This love makes havock with man, woman, and child! tho', of a truth, the paffion is fomewhat blunted in me, fince I left Tiperary.

SONG.

KILMALLOCK.

At fixteen years old you could get little good
    of me;
Then I faw Norah,—who foon underftood of
    me,
I was in love—but myfelf, for the blood of me,
    Could not tell what I did ail.
  Twas dear, dear! whan can the matter be!
Och! blood an ouns! what can the matter be!
Och, Gramachree! what can the matter be!
    Bother'd from head to the tail.

I went to confefs me to Father O'Flannagan;
Told him my cafe—made an end—then began
    again:—
Father, fays I, make me foon my own man again,
    If you find out what I ail.
  Dear, dear! fays he, what can the matter be!
Och! blood an ouns! can't you tell what the
    matter be?
  Both cried out, what can the matter be!
    Bother'd from head to the tail.

Soon I fell fick—I did bellow and curfe again.—
Norah took pity to fee me at nurfe again:

                         Gave

Gave me a kifs;—Och, zounds! that threw me
    worfe again!
  Well, fhe knew what I did ail:—
But, dear, dear! fays fhe, what can the matter
    be!
Och, blood an ouns! my lafs, what can the
    matter be!
Both cried out what can the matter be!
    Bother'd from head to the tail.

'Tis long ago now fince I left Tiperary.—
How ftrange, growing older, our nature fhould
    vary!
All fymptoms are gone of my ancient quandary—
  I cannot tell *now* what I ail.
Dear, dear, what can the matter be!
Och, blood an ouns! what can the matter be!
Och, Gramachree! what can the matter be!
    I'm bother'd from head to the tail. [*Exit.*

SCENE III. *Another part of the Sierra de Ronda. In one part of the Scene, a cave overgrown with bufhes: in another, a rude bank, with ftumps of trees.* (Day-break.)

Enter two GOATHERDS.

GOATHERD.

See, yonder, where day peeps. Here is the cave, father; hang your wine-cag at the mouth on't, and then away to tend our goats.

GOATHERD.

Poor Gentleman! a fup on't may cheer his heart. (*Hangs the cag at the mouth of the cave.*)
    "Tis

Tis sorry lodging to be tenant of this cave for a twelvemonth, as he has been; and trust to Providence, and us Goatherds, for board. That a civil, well-favour'd Cavalier, should come to this pass!

Diego.

Civil! plague on him! When a'met me, i'the dusk, as a'straggled a league from this, a'snatch'd a brown loaf from my hand, and gave me a shower of thwacks on the shoulders for payment.

Pablo.

Alas! boy, that was in his mood;—his melancholy.—'Twill, as thou know'st, trouble him sore at times; but it rarely lasts.

Diego.

Flesh! I know 'twill at times trouble others—and the soreness lasts a week after it. What affairs should call a melancholy Gentleman, like him, to our wild mountains?

Pablo.

Diego, I do think I have hit on't.—I do think 'tis love has put him beside himself. Ask thy mother, boy, when she cross'd me in wooing, how I would sometimes start from reason.

Diego.

'Troth, father, you have that trick still. I fear me, you have been ill cured.

Pablo.

Out graceless!—Hush!—dost not hear him stir?

1st. GOAT-

~~GOATHERD~~ DIEGO.

Nay, then— ~~come~~ away father; and leave your
charity behind you!—an he should be in his
mood now, we might as well meet the devil.
Run, old man, or Melancholy will cudgel thee.—
Away, father! Away!   [*Exeunt R*

Enter OCTAVIAN.   (*from the Cave.*)

OCTAVIAN.

I cannot sleep.—The leaves are newly pull'd;
And, as my burning body presses them,
Their freshness mocks my misery.—That frets
    me—
And then I could outwatch the lynx. 'Tis
    dawn.—
Thou hot and rolling Sun! I rise before thee!
For I have twice thy scorching flames within
    me,
And am more restless. Now to seek my willow—
That droops his mournful head across the brook:
He is my calendar; I'll score his trunk,
With one more long, long day of solitude!
I shall lose count, else, in my wretchedness;
And that were pity.———Oh, Octavian!
Where are the times thy ardent nature painted,
When fortune smil'd upon thy lusty youth,
And all was sunshine?—Where the look'd-for
    years,
Gaily bedeck'd with fancy's imagery,
When the high blood ran frolick through thy
    veins,
And boyhood made thee sanguine?—Let them
    vanish—
Prosperity's a cheat—Despair is honest;
And will stick by me, steadily—I'll hug it—

Will glut on't—why the greybeard tore her from
  me,
Even in my foul's fond dotage. O! tis paftime
To fee men, now, tug at each other's hearts:
I fear not—for my ftrings are crack'd already.
I will go prowl—but look I meet no fathers.
Now, willow!—O, Floranthe! [*Exit R*

—Enter SADI *and* AGNES.

SADI.

A plague on all horfes, mountains, and quag-
mires;—nay, keep a good heart, Agnes! Of all
the roads to Chriftianity this is the vileft that ever
good fellow travel'd. How fares it, Agnes?

AGNES.

O, Sadi! I fhall never live through this mountain.

SADI.

Nay, I warrant we'll do well. Do not flag—Do
not give way, thus, for my fake. Confider I muft
fupport you, Agnes,—and, to fee you thus, I can
fcarce fupport myfelf. I have had my load of vexa-
tion ere now—but this is the firft time I ever car-
ried double; and I know not well how to bear it.

AGNES.

Good faith, I do my beft, Sadi—and I have one
comfort left me, ftill.

SADI.

Aye, I warrant—what is it, Agnes.?

AGNES.

Why you are with me, Sadi—fhould fatigue
wear me, and fhould I die in thefe wilds, you
would clofe the eyes of your poor Agnes;—
                                                and

and I should go in peace, with one near me who has been so faithful to me.

SADI.

No, truly, Agnes, I could never do thee that office. Close thy eyes!—I should have so much need to lift the napkin to my own, I could never see to perform it. What, thou art not faint, Agnes?

AGNES.

Trust me, very faint, Sadi:—and sick—sick at heart.

SADI.

With fasting, poor soul! These mountains would teaze hunger into a fever: there are eatables perch'd upon every bush, but not a morsel that is'n't alive.

AGNES.

Fainter, and fainter!

SADI.

Rest you on this clump, Agnes—and if any thing may be found near us, to comfort thee, I'll fight for it through a—ch! a Cave! and a cag hung at the mouth on't. *(takes it down).* Wine, by the Koran! To see what Providence will do for a Christian! Were a Musselman fainting to death, this is the first thing Mahomet would kick out of his way. Drink, drink, Agnes! and much good may it do thy little heart! *(holds the cag to her mouth.)* How dost now?

AGNES.

Sooth it has cheered me;—but—

SADI.

Well?

AGNES.

Will not you drink, too, Sadi?

SADI.

Now does confcience make a ftir within me, to know whether I am qualified to fup this liquor, or not. Doft think, Agnes, I am Chriftian enough, yet to venture? ~~I travel in a gap here, between two perfuafions, till I fhall fhortly fall to the ground.~~

AGNES.

Go to, man, thou need'ft it; and there is much virtue in good wine.

SADI.

Nay, an there be virtue in't—*(drinks)* by Saint Francis, Agnes, thy religion is marvellous comfortable! Would we were fafe fettled in Andalufia! I fhall make as chopping a fubject for a chriftening as ever nurfe put into the hands of a Friar. Can'ft journey onward think you, Agnes?

AGNES.

Shall we overtake the Lady Zorayda?

SADI.

Nay, that's hopelefs. We are bewildered here, in the woods;—and muft e'en give up thoughts of feeing her, till we reach Seville.

AGNES.

Heaven fend the dear lady be fafe! I would fain

5 Ulysses goes to the mouth of the Cave

fain then reſt me, Sadi : for in footh, my legs fail me ſadly.

SADI.

And here ſtands a cave, yawning as it would invite ſleep. In, Agnes, and I'll keep guard. ~~Truly, though the ſheets be leaves, they promiſe to be well air'd; for they bear the print of one who has lately ſlept in them.~~

AGNES.

You will not quit me, now?

SADI.

I would quit life firſt. Should any venture to harm thee, they muſt taſte what a Moor's dagger be made of. *(Puts Agnes into the cave.)*

Enter OCTAVIAN.

OCTAVIAN.

How now!

SADI.

Here is one willing to taſte already. This, now, by the coſtlineſs of his robes, muſt be lord of this manſion. What would you?

OCTAVIAN.

I would paſs—
Deep in yon cave, to hide me from the ſun:
His riſing beams have tipt the trees with gold—
He gladdens men—but I do baſk in ſorrow.
Give way!——

SADI.

Mark you—I do reſpect ſorrow too much to do it wilful injury. I am a Moor 'tis true—that
is

is, I am not quite a Christian—but I never yet
saw man bending under misfortune, that I did
not think it pleasure to lighten his load. Strive
to pass here, and I must add blows to *your* burthen;—and that might haply break your back:—
for, to say truth, I have now a treasure in this
cave, that, while I can hinder it, sorrow shall
never come nigh.

OCTAVIAN.

Death! must I burrow here with brutes, and
 find
My haunts broke in upon! my cares disturb'd!
Reptile! I'll dash thy body o'er the rocks,
And leave thee to the vultures.

SADI.

Friend, you'll find me too tough to be serv'd
up to 'em. An they must dine upon one of us,
we will see which will afford them a picking.
 *(They struggle.—Agnes rushes from the cave
 between them.)*

AGNES.

O, Sadi;—for my sake!—Gentleman!—hold!

OCTAVIAN.

Woman!

SADI.

Aye; and touch her at your peril.

OCTAVIAN.

Not for the worth of worlds. Thou lovest her?--
 Mark—
He who would cut the knot that does entwine,
And link two loving hearts in unison,
 May

May have man's form;—but at his birth,—be
    sure on't---
Some devil thrust sweet Nature's hand aside,
Ere she had pour'd her balm within his breast,
To warm his gross and earthy mould with pity.

SADI.

This fellow now is like a great melon:—with a rough outside, and much sweetness under it. It seems as thou wert sent ragged Embassador, here, from a strange nation, to treat with the four-foot citizens of this mountain:—and as we are unknown in these parts, we will e'en throw ourselves on thy protection.

OCTAVIAN.

Some paces hence, there is a goatherd's cot,
Begirt with brake, and bush—and weather proof—

AGNES.

Let us thither, Sadi.

SADI.

Content.

OCTAVIAN.

I'll lead thee to't; for I am high in office
In Cupid's cabinet:—I bear the torch
Before the little god; and 'tis my care
To shield from peril true love's votaries.

SADI.

I knew he was a great man—but I never heard mention before of such a place of dignity. Along, good fellow! and we'll follow thee.

OCTAVIAN.

OCTAVIAN.

They fhall not part you:---for I know what 'tis
When worldly knaves ftep in, with filver beards,
To poifon blifs, and pluck young fouls afunder.---
O! wander, boundlefs love, acrofs the wild!
Give thy free paffion fcope, and range the wil-
  dernefs!
Crib not thyfelf in cities---for 'tis there
The thrifty, grey philofopher inhabits,
To check thy glowing impulfe in his child.
Gain is the old man's god; he offers up
His iffue to't;---and mercenary wedlock
Murders his offspring's peace.---they murdered
  mine---
They tore it from my bofom by the roots,
And with it, pluck'd out hope! Well, well, no
  matter---
Defpair burns high within me, and it's fire
Serves me for heart, to keep my clay in motion.---
Follow my footfteps.

AGNES.

Out, alas! his wits are turn'd. Do not venture with him, Sadi; he will do us a mifchief.

SADI.

Truly the tenement of his brain feems fomewhat out of repair; yet, if he brings you to a
place of fafety, Agnes—I know not whether we
fhould take this crazy Gentleman as a guide, or
truft to reafon;---which, indeed, is but a poor
director of the road when a man has loft his way.
Wilt lead us fafe, now?

OCTAVIAN.

..Be fure on't.

SADI.

THE MOUNTAINEERS. 57

SADI.

Tuck thyfelf under my arm, Agnes. Now out fcymetar!—Bring us to this fame Goatherd's, and thou fhalt have the beft acknowledgments gratitude can give thee. If thou ventureft to harm *her (pointing to Agnes)* I'll quickly ftir the fire in thy bofom thou talkeft of, and this fhall ferve for the poker.   *(fhewing his fcymetar.)*

OCTAVIAN.

Should the gaunt wolf crofs lovers in their path,
I'd rend his rugged jaws; and he fhould bay
The moon' no more, with howling. Thread the
    thicket——
Follow love's meffenger. *Come &c.*   [*Exeunt*

Enter Goatherds, and Spanifh paftoral characters, male and female.

3rd GOATHERD.

On brother Goatherds! by the mafs, 'tis broad day! and the blazing fun cries fluggard upon us. Up to the pens; our goats will choak elfe—they have needed drink an hour ago.

4th GOATHERD.

Troth, brother, and fo have we. When man has a call for refrefhment, 'tis but fit beaft fhould tarry 'till his better be ferv'd before him. We have walk'd a good half league from home—let us wet our whiftles, and then we will think on the horns and long beards of our old cuckoldy cattle.

I   SONG

Song *and* Chorus *of* Goatherds.

1st MAN.
Brother Goatherd, mark you me?
Pledge me, when I drink to thee.
Let us drain the skins of wine,
Till our ruby noses shine.
Mountain grapes, and mountain cheer,
Warm the merry Mountaineer.

2nd MAN.
Let us push the wine about,
Till the last, last drop is out:
Then each Spanish man go
And dance the Fandango,
When jigging with lasses,
How sweet the time passes,
When mountain grapes, and mountain cheer,
Have warm'd the merry Mountaineer!

WOMAN.
Sluggish Goatherds, haste away!
The drooping cattle mourn your stay.
Labour, 'till the sloping sun
Tells you that your work is done;
Then your rough brows with chaplets
  deck,
And trimly dance to the rebeck:
Then each Spanish man go
And move the Fandango—
When jigging with lasses,
How sweet the time passes!
When work is done, and mountain cheer
Warms the merry Mountaineer! [*Exeunt*

END OF ACT II.

ACT III.

SCENE I. *The Sierra de Ronda.*

Enter BULCAZIN MULEY, GANEM, *and Moorish Soldiers.*

GANEM.

IN truth the men muſt reſt, Sir.

BULCAZIN.

Muſt!

GANEM.

Perforce.
This long, and hurried march, has made them faint.
We are all nigh to drop.

BULCAZIN.

Here ſink and rot, then—I will on alone—
Sluggard! the bliſters, now, that gall thy feet,
Work upward to thy heart, and feſter there—
Then thou wilt feel ſome touch of anguiſh in't,
Like that which thou haſt fixed in mine. Thou baſe,
Unmindful ſlave! who, in thy maſter's abſence,
Should'ſt mark each fly that buzzes through his portal,
Thy vigilance muſt nod upon its poſt,
While a vile Chriſtian ſteals away my daughter.

GANEM.

GANEM.

Believe me, Sir——

BULCAZIN.

I will not, wretch, believe thee.
Thou art—Yes, Ganem, yes I will believe thee.
'Twas all my daughter's doing—'twas her nature;
Her sex's wicked, wanton, subtle nature.
Sure our wise Prophet thought his followers fools,
When he first promis'd Woman for their paradise.
Collect the wide world's womanhood together,
And the huge zone that does encompass them
Will bind up half the plagues that vex mankind:
Heap them into a bulk, their airy falsehood
Would poise a solid universe. To fly me!
To fly her father—and so kind a father!
If somewhat rough—that was the trick of battles
Where I was bred—She knew I doated on her—
When I have thought on what would charm the
    sense,
Till it would almost ache with tenderness,
Great Alla knows, I have named thee Zorayda!
Then leave me thus—and break my poor old
    heart!
And with a Christian too—Oh death and shame!
Should she now cross me, though she smil'd upon
    me,
Like twenty dimpled Cherubims, my rage
Would tear her limb from limb, and her sweet
    form
Should scatter piece-meal thro' the desart.

GANEM.

Sir,
I pray you be advised: think what is best
To cheer your fainting people on the march.—
                         Your

Your pardon, Sir, but this same flow of passion,
Unnerving you, and harassing your men,
Defeats the purpose of your enterprise.

BULCAZIN.

Check my full passion! happy, happy fool!
Thou knowest not a fond parent's agony,
Deserted by his loved, ungrateful child,
O, my Zorayda! dear, shameless girl!
Thou art delicious poison to my sense,
Most sweet, and yet most deadly.   Out upon
    thee!
To wind thee, like a snake, about my heart,
And sting as thou dost twine there. I could stab
    thee,
In stern and rugged justice; and affection
Would throw the weeping father on his knees,
To kiss the wound the much wrong'd judge had
    made.

GANEM.

Beseech you, Sir, give order for your soldiery.

BULCAZIN.

A pestilence upon thee! thou'rt a fiend
That grudgest me my sorrow's luxury,
And goad'st me when I would indulge on torture.
Tell me, again, of what these filth endure,
I'll cleave thy body, downward, from thy head,
To teach them how to labour, and be silent.

GANEM.

Think, Sir, it is in care alone for you
I pour unpleasing truth into your ear;
Which, like a nauseous drug to the diseased,
Is given to work your welfare. 'Tis my duty—
Sooth, Sir, they cannot on.

BULCAZIN.

BULCAZIN.

Mad, fenfelefs liar!
Thou gallest me paft endurance; and haft pulled
Thy death upon thee.   *(Draws his fcymetar.*

GANEM.—*(Kneeling)*.

O, Sir, take my life!
It is not worth the keeping—I have follow'd you,
From infancy till now, in honeft zeal—
'Twould grieve me, Sir, to feek another mafter;
And, as my truth is grown difpleafing to you,
'Twere beft you bring my fervice to a clofe,
And e'en difpatch me here, at once.

BULCAZIN.—*(Softened)*.

Why, Ganem—
I tell thee Ganem—Pfhaw! when we are form'd
So much of mother marks our compofition,
It mars our manly refolution.—Ganem,
I have a daughter—think on that, good Ganem?
And fhe has fled me—I do think thy counfel
Is kindly meant—but fpare it now, good fellow,
My paffions cannot brook it.—Have we ftray'd?
Do we purfue their track?

GANEM.

The peafant, Sir,
Whom we did queftion, at the mountain's foot,
Pointed this path to Ronda. Thitherward
Your daughter, as we trace it, muft have
   journey'd.

BULCAZIN.

They fhall not reft. Have I not fhared their
   labour?
He who firft murmurs on his march, dies for it.
By Mahomet, I fwear! if I do hear

A fingle

A single Moor bewailing the fatigue
His coward body suffers, on the instant,
My scymetar shall search his body through!
March slaves! away!

[Exeunt L.

SCENE II. *The outside of a Goatherd's cottage.*

SADI *and* AGNES *discovered before the door at a table, eating and drinking.*

SADI.

Truly, eating is a mighty refreshing invention! This Olla Podrida of our friend the goatherd's, here, has a strange quality in't of raising the spirits. What is the reason on't Agnes? I never swallowed a meal before that made me so merry.

AGNES.

Out, you goose! 'tis the wine that thou hast drank. Wine thou knowest comforts man, and makes him light of heart, Sadi.

SADI.

What an advantage 'tis to a Catholic to be able thus to cork up comfort, and carry his happiness about with him, under his arm in a flaggon. —Pour some of this light-heartedness down thy sweet throat, Agnes. Had I a hundred vintages of welfare, I would leave them all untapped, if thou wert not by to share them with me.

(Fill and drink.)

AGNES.

AGNES.

'Tis sufficient, Sadi. *(rise.)* Thou knoweft not the ftrength of liquor—too much on't would work to thy brain, and weaken reafon.

SADI.

That muft be becaufe my fkull is not, yet, altogether Chriftian. It could never happen to a regular head to grow weak with having ftrength cram'd into it.—Did'ft repofe well here, at the Goatherd's, Agnes?

AGNES.

Truft me, did I—but it had better pleafed me had not you fat and watch'd, in the corner of the hut, while I refted.

SADI.

I could watch twenty years like a cat, to fee you fleep fo fweetly. What a pretty thing it is to be near the woman one loves when fhe's taking a nap! and check one's inclinations of kiffing her eyelids, for fear of awaking her!—Should'ft thou ever flumber at night with thy head upon my fhoulder, Agnes, I wouldn't ftir to difturb thee, though I were bit all over by a million of mufquitos.

AGNES.

Away, you giddy pate!—Thou wilt be a right follower of the bottle fhortly—when the liquor mounts, then thou wilt flatter me—and prate nonfenfe, like the beft Chriftian toper of them all.

SADI.

Why look thee, fweet! Ere I loved a bottle— I loved a woman.—And I am told he that fticks fairly

3.

(a)

~~fairly to the one, seldom behaves like a knave to the other.~~—My love for wine is but of a few hours growth—yet though I was enamour'd at firſt taſte, I mean to ſtick by it with true Chriſtian conſtancy—for it has let me into a ſecret, Agnes,—ev'ry drop I take of it, makes me find out how much delight I have in thy company---I grow fonder and fonder at every tipple.

AGNES.

Aye; ſo it would happen were any *other* preſent but I.

SADI.

No, by Mahom——piſh, that's a Muſſelman oath--and diſgraces a mouth that has been waſh'd with wine---by Saint Dominick! then, ſweet Agnes,—ſhould all the beauties of Spain be collected together like a huge row of filberts, I would pick thee from the cluſter, nor think another nut in the whole grove worth the cracking.

AGNES.

Will thy love hold faſt, now, after we are married, Sadi?

SADI.

Aye, marry, will it, and never let go. 'Tis in my nature, wench. You might as ſoon think to ſcour me white as ſcrub my love out of me. 'Tis of the laſting kind, Agnes, like my countenance. ~~Mine is your true paſſion in grain—and will ſtand it's colour at all ſeaſons.~~

AGNES.

And, if thy ſkin grows duſky as thy love ſtrengthens, Sadi, I ſhould think thee pretty, though thy cheeks were as dark as a raven.

K   SADI.

SADI.

There is no accounting for the taste of a female. Were all women of thy mind, Agnes, what a number of vain, copper-faced gentlemen would strut about among the girls in Christian countries. We should frisk it through the towns, as merry as dogs in a market—and dingy puppies would be as plenty as those of a lighter complexion.—Shall we into the hut, and look to our poor crazy guide here?

AGNES.

O, Sadi, my heart bleeds for him! He will sit awhile, and look stedfastly on nothing—and then groan as piteous, as though 'twould rive his very body. Would we could comfort him!

SADI.

I will pour a flask of wine down his throat—an' that comfort him not, he is past cure in this world, and must look elsewhere for consolation.

DUET.
Sadi *and* Agnes.

1.

Faint, and wearily, the way-worn traveller
Plods, uncheerily, afraid to stop!
Wand'ring, drearily, a sad unraveller
Of the mazes tow'rd the mountain's top!
    Doubting, fearing,
    While his course he's steering—
    Cottages appearing,
    When he's nigh to drop—
O! how briskly, then, the way-worn traveller
Threads the mazes tow'rd the mountain's top!

II. Though

☉ Crotophaga b~

II.

Though so melancholy day has past by,
'Twould be folly, now, to think on't more:—
Blythe, and jolly, he the keg holds fast by,
As he's sitting at the goatherd's door:
    Eating, quaffing,
    At past labour laughing!
    Better, far, by half, in
    Spirits than before—
O! how merry, then, the rested traveller
Seems, while sitting at the goatherd's door!

SADI.

Who comes here?

(Enter FLORANTHE *and* ROQUE*).*

ROQUE.

Stand.

SADI.

Not the sooner for thy bidding—But when a blustering knave cries, Stand! I hold him to be little better than a cowardly fool that thinks of running away.

ROQUE.

Art not a Moor, and an enemy?

SADI.

I have now near two full flagons of Christianity within me, but I am somewhat Moorish as to impatience—therefore parley courteously, lest you get nothing but dry blows in exchange.

FLORANTHE.

Peace, peace, good Roque—and let me question him.

Tell

Tell me, beseech you, as you journeyed on,
Has it so chanc'd that there should cross your path
A man—good faith, it cuts my heart in twain
How to describe him.

SADI.

What kind of man?

FLORANTHE.

Lovely as day he was—but envious clouds
Have dim'd his lustre. He is as a rock,
Oppos'd to the rude sea that beats against it;
Worn by the waves, yet, still o'ertopping them,
In sullen majesty.—Rugged, now, his look—
For out, alas! Calamity has blur'd
The fairest pile of manly comeliness,
That ever rear'd its lofty head to heaven!
'Tis not of late that I have heard his voice;
But if it be not changed—I think it cannot—
There is a melody, in ev'ry tone,
Would charm the tow'ring eagle in her flight,
And tame a hungry lion.

AGNES.

Never trust me, Sadi, if he means not our guide.

SADI.

Answer me to one point, and I can satisfy you.— ~~Will he fly at a man that keeps him three seconds out of an ill-made bed?~~—Is he crazy?

ROQUE.

Crazy!—Now do my fingers itch to beat this unmannerly morsel of dinginess.

SADI.

Hark ye, rough Sir—Should occasion serve, I can go to cuffs with as good will as another.

FLORANTHE.

Prithee be calm, Roque—Now to anfwer thee—
He whom we feek—thro' wayward circumftance,
And croffes of the time,—tho', in the main,
His reafon is moft clear—will in fome fort—
(We learn it on the fkirts here of the mountain)
Start into paffion—and his matter, then,—
Tho' method ever tempers his difcourfe,—
May feem, I fear, to thofe who know him not,
Like idle phantafy.

SADI.

Truly, fuch a ~~defcription might fuit this fiery gentleman, your~~ follower,—who f.. ts into paf~~fion with little or no caufe.—But fuch a~~ man have
I feen—fuch a man, in pure kindnefs, has conducted us hither—and fuch a man is now within,
in the hut here.

FLORANTHE.

Here!—Mercy, heaven!

ROQUE.

Nay, nay, bear up, lady! Our labour now
will ~~foon have an end~~—All will be well, I warrant; lead us in, my good fellow!

SADI.

Good fellow! This is one of your weathercock
knaves, now, that point always as the wind veers.
~~A fudden puff of my information has blown him round to civility. (Afide)~~.—In, and ~~I'll conduct~~
you.—We muft wait awhile, however, in the
outward nook of the hovel:—for to thruft ourfelves fuddenly into the prefence of fo moody a
gentleman, might haply offend his dignity. ~~Come, Agnes.~~

AGNES.

Have with you, Sadi.

SADI.

Nay, I would not budge an inch without thee, sweet!—In, young Sir, and I'll shew thee.

FLORANTHE.

Lead—and we'll follow,

ROQUE.

Pray ye, be of good heart.

FLORANTHE.

Well, well—I tremble sadly!

[*Exeunt.*

SCENE III. *Inside of a Goatherd's cottage.*

Enter OCTAVIAN *and a Goatherd.*

GOATHERD.

Neither food nor repose! well, 'tis strange! will nothing persuade you to take refreshment, gentle Sir?

OCTAVIAN.

Nothing that thou can'st say.—Why thou art old:
And 'tis the trick of age to proffer gifts,
Merely to teize the wretch that would accept them.

GOATHERD.

Nay, by our lady!

OCTAVIAN.

Jack. Come, Agnes.
Agnes. Have with you, Jack.
Jack. Nay I would not budge an inch without thee, sweet
I say, Agnes, this snug little Cabin of the Goatherd's
with good cheer and excellent Malaga is better
than Tendgnio over the Mountains, with tired legs
and empty stomachs.

        Duett:-
Faint and wearily &c. (See Page 6)

            Exeunt into Cottage.

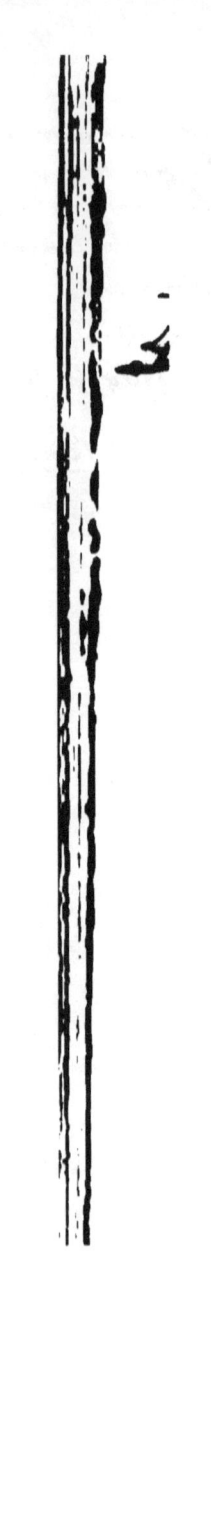

OCTAVIAN.

Hark ye—ere now, there came a hoary cheat,
And placed before my eyes the richeſt fare
That ever tempted glutton:—What do'ſt think?
When I would taſte, he whipt it from the board,
And thruſt me forth to ſtarve:—but he was
    fool'd:
For then I drank huge draughts of ſorrow down,
And banqueted on tears.

Maſs! 'twas a ſorry method of regaling! were
I given to revelry, I would look for liquor of
another brewage.

OCTAVIAN.

Thou'dſt look for any thing to ſwell thy ſtore,
Tho' thy full bags were burſting. Were the road
To one poor ducat paved with youthful hearts,
Sprinkle grey hairs upon a fellow's pate,
He'd trample o'er them all, to catch at it.
Where are thy children?

I have but one—one only daughter—and alas!
ſhe has gone I know not whither! Pedro had had
my conſent to woo her, had he not been altogether
poor; and now ſhe has ſtray'd away in deſpair,
becauſe I would not ſee her wed unhappily.

OCTAVIAN.

Why 'twas well done.—'Twas juſtice on thy
    avarice,
To doom thyſelf to living purgatory;
And fix without thy breaſt the gnawing thought
                                       That

That thou haſt driven forth thy innocent child,
Through the wide globe, a friendleſs wanderer.
O, thou wilt thrive, now, in the ſhuffling croud
Of this world's traffick!—When the drover comes,
Sell him thy rotten goats, and rate them ſound
As thoſe of higheſt market.—Cheat thy neigh-
　　bour ;
Fleece him, and fear not ;—glut thyſelf on plunder ;
For thou art ſunk ſo low in hell, for this,
There is no guilt in vice's catalogue,
Can plunge thee deeper.
See who 'tis that knocks.　　[*A knocking without.*]

GOATHERD.

　　I will, Sir;—but I am not as you would picture
me, for all your ſaying. I have not lived forty
years, on the credit of my cattle, to offer rotten
rams for ſale, at this time of day, and paſs them
current.—I ſhall to the door, Sir.　　[*Exit.*

OCTAVIAN. *(pulls a portrait from his boſom.)*
　　Out bauble!—let me kiſs thee!—ſweet Flo-
　　ranthe!
When the cold Limner drew thy ſemblance here,
How charm'd I ſat, to mark the modeſt fluſh
That virgin nature threw into thy face,
As the dull clod unmoved did ſtare upon thee,
To pencil out thy features' character!
Thoſe times are paſt, Floranthe!—yet 'tis comfort
To bring remembrance full upon the eye :—
'Tis ſoothing, to a fond, and care-worn heart,
To drop a tear on the loved lineaments
Of her it ne'er muſt hope to meet again!

—Enter ROQUE.

ROQUE.

　　Now know not I how to accoſt him. Poor
　　　　　　　　　　　　　　　　　　gentleman!

gentleman! Times are sadly changed with him, since I saw him fresh, and well caparisoned, gazing on my young lady, in my old master's mansion, at Seville. I do not, altogether think my heart is tough enough for my trade:—it has too many soft places in it, and the misfortunes of another are apt to take the advantage of them; and disable me from fighting through the rough work of the world with firmness—Signior! Signior! do you not remember my countenance?

OCTAVIAN.

No—Providence has slubber'd it in haste.
'Tis one of her unmeaning compositions
She manufactures when she makes a grofs.
She'll form a million such—and all alike—
Then send them forth, ashamed of her own work,
And set no mark upon them. Get thee gone.

ROQUE.

Get me gone!—Ah! Signior! the time has been when you would question old Roque kindly after his health, as he lifted up the latch to give you admittance to poor Donna Floranthe.

OCTAVIAN.

Thou hast shot lightning through me!—Art thou—stay!—
That sound was thrilling musick! O, Floranthe!
I thought not e'en the magick of thy name
Could make a heart, so long benumb'd with misery,
Leap as 'twould burst its prison.—Do not mock me;
If thou dost juggle, now, I'll tear thee——Hold!
Aye, I remember;—and as I peruse thee,
Past times rush in upon me, with thy face;

And many a thought of happiness, gone by,
Does flash across my brain.   Let me not wander
Give me thy hand, Roque.---I do know thy
    errand:
And 'tis of import, when thou journey'st, thus,
The trackless desart to seek sorrow out.
Thou comest to tell me my Floranthe's dead :—
But we will meet again, sweet!---I will back,
With thee, old honesty; and lay me down,
Heart-broke, at last, beside her shrouded corse,
Kiss her cold cheek, then fly to her in heaven!

ROQUE.

I would I were in the midst of a battle—I
know not how 'tis—I have faced many a man in
the field; but this is an engagement that makes
my spirits sink down to my very heels, I do verily
believe my courage, in my old age, begins to
dwindle.

OCTAVIAN.

Tell me, old Roque! tell me Floranthe's fol-
    lower!
Shall we not, when the midnight bell has toll'd,
Beguile the drunken sacrist of his key?
Then steal in silence, up the church's aile,
To sprinkle Cypress on her monument.

ROQUE.

An this hold, I shall blubber outright, like a
female baby. I must muster my own resolution
that I may rally his.—Why, how now, Signior
shame on this weakness!—were all to bend like
you, when they meet disappointment, I know
not who in this justling life would walk upright
Pluck

4 Oct:- Oh!-

Pluck up your manly spirits, Signior! your Floranthe lives—aye, and is true to you—now, by Saint Dominick I bring tidings that will glad you.

OCTAVIAN.

I pray you, do not sport with me, old man—
Jeer not the wretched—I have worn away
Twelve weary months in anguish: I have sat,
Darkling, by day in caverns—and, at night,
Have fix'd my eyes so long upon the moon,
That I do fear my senses are, in part,
Sway'd by her influence. I'm past jesting with.

ROQUE.

I never, Signior, was much given to jesting—and he who sports with the misfortunes of another, though he may bring his head into repute for fancy, does his heart little credit for feeling. I had rather be accounted a well-disposed dullard, than an excellent-witted knave.— Rest you quiet, Signior!—Here is one waiting without, that I have brought along with me, who will comfort you. Nay, I pray you, now, be patient—If this be the work of bringing lovers together, heaven give him joy who makes a trade on't! for in fifty years that Time has clapp'd his saddle on my back, he never so sorely gall'd my old withers as now. [*Exit L.D.*

OCTAVIAN.

Habit does much—I do begin to think,
Since Grief has been so close an inmate with me,
That I have strain'd her nearer to my bosom
Than I *had* press'd her, had the chequer'd scene,
Which rouses man, who mixes with his kind,
Kept me from dotage on her.—Our affections

Muſt have a reſt—and ſorrow, when ſecluded,
Grows ſtrong in weakneſs.—Pen the body up,
In ſolitary durance, and, in time,
The human ſoul will idly fix its fancy
E'en on ſome peg, ſtuck in the priſon's wall,
And ſigh to quit it.—Sure I am not mad!—
Floranthe's loſt—and ſince his ſtubborn frame
Will ſtand the tug—I'll to the heated world—
Fit mingler in the throng, miſcall'd Society.

(Enter Floranthe).

(*A pauſe—He gazes on her for ſome time*).

What art thou?—ſpeak——that face—yet this attire—
Floranthe!—No—It cannot—Oh! good heaven!
Vex not a poor weak creature thus! Floranthe?
How my ſight thickens—Speak—

FLORANTHE.

Octavian!

OCTAVIAN.

That voice!—It is—So long too!—Let me claſp thee—

(*Runs to meet her—ſtaggers—and falls on his face*).

FLORANTHE.

O, I did fear this—my Octavian—
To ſee thee thus!—Why, Roque—Alas, Octa-
vian,
Revive, or thou wilt kill me—'Tis Floranthe,
Thy own Floranthe——

Enter ROQUE, (*who aſſiſts* OCTAVIAN.)

OCTAVIAN (*recovering*).

It has chanced, before,
That I have dreamt this—and, when I awoke,

for Roque & Floranthe
points out Octavian to Floranthe.
& L.D.

& Floranthe is much terrified — Rogue & behind to

Big drops did stand upon my clay-cold front,
As they do now, the vision did so shake me.
'Tis there again—Brain! brain! Why, aye, that
    hand—
Pray let me kiss it—O, 'tis she!—'Tis real—
For my strong pulse is still so sensible
To ev'ry touch of thine, that the sweet contact
Strikes certain to it; and now it throbs intelli-
    gence.
How comes this?—are you here to scoff me, lady?
Alas, Floranthe, I am sadly chang'd
Since last we parted!

FLORANTHE.

Scoff thee, Octavian! Ah, thou little know'st
How often I have wept away the night
With thinking on thy fortunes—but, alas!
I ne'er thought this!—O! what hast thou endur'd!
Wand'ring, expos'd, unshelter'd!

OCTAVIAN.

That's nothing—
I heeded not the storm:— I remember,
When last the forked lightning struck me down,
I lay upon the rock, and smil'd to see
The feeble malice of the elements.
'Tis here,—here only, I am vulnerable.
    (Pointing to his breast.)
I have been gall'd too deep within, Floranthe,
To think upon the petty sufferance
Felt by a holiday and silken fool,
When the rough tempest beats upon his body.

FLORANTHE.

You cut my heart across. Pray you, be com-
    forted;
                                 I will

I will pour balm into thy bleeding wounds,
And heal them up for ever.

    OCTAVIAN.

       Get thee back—
He who would snatch thee from me, tho' he fell,
(Fell by this arm)—met not his death by me:
(I had not fled three days ere I did learn it)
And sure thy father, whose delight it is
To torture faithful love, has giv'n thee to him.
The thought does mad me; get thee to thy hus-
  band.

    FLORANTHE.

Then let me greet him here—for here, Octavian,
In firm and maiden holiness, I swear,
If *thou* dost never lead me to the altar,
My life shall waste in cloister'd solitude;
And when the passing-bell proclaims me dead,
Our convent's votarists will chaunt their dirge,
To grace a virgin sister's funeral.

    OCTAVIAN.

How's this?—What has thy father then—im-
  possible!—
Does he relent?

    FLORANTHE.

    Alas! he is no more;
(I needs must grieve, for still he was my father)
And he who stood between thy love and thee,
Is wedded to another.

    OCTAVIAN.

    Art thou mine, then!
    (Bursts into hysterical laughter)
Sir, I am very weak:—pray pardon me,
'Tis somewhat sudden this—I am unused
          To

1 { Oct. throws Flor. from him — She runs to Rogue, who is R.

2 { Flor. advances towards Octa. as if going to assure him that his suspicions are groundless.

3 { Octa. falls into Rogue's arms. Flor. is greatly agitated, which Rogue observing, he, as soon as Octa. quits him, goes behind to her L. and endeavours to comfort her.

THE MOUNTAINEERS.   79

To any touch of joy, and it o'ercomes [powers] me.
I shall weep soon, and then I shall be better.

FLORANTHE.

Nay, calm thy spirits—prithee now—

OCTAVIAN.

      Well, well.—
Look on me, sweet! my own beloved Floranthe!
O! many a time, in anguish, have I brought
That angel form before my fancy's eye,
'Till my hot brain has driv'n me thro' the wild,
Daring, by night, the precipice's edge,
To clasp thy airy phantom. This repays me.
O! plunge me, deep, in Ætna's smoky gulph;
And I could wallow, calmly, in her fires,
Like lazy shepherds basking in the sun,
To hold thee thus at last!

FLORANTHE.

Restrain this passion.
These starts do wear thee sadly. *We will leave this gloom*

OCTAVIAN.

Come— Let us on. — — *Exit Rogue L.D.*
As I do cool, I shudder at myself;
And look, with horror, back, upon this waste,
Where, cheerless, I have stray'd, shut out from man,
A solitary wild inhabitant. *{Floranthe points to the door}*
x L. Have with thee, sweet! I know each turn and thicket.
Already I have felt what 'tis to lose thee:
They take my life who tear thee from me now;
For death alone shall part us. Come Floranthe!
        [*Exeunt L.D.*

SCENE

SCENE IV. *The Sierra de Ronda.*

Enter VIROLET, ZORAYDA, *and* KILMALLOCK.

VIROLET.

I tell thee, thou doſt lead us wrong, Kilmallock.
See, here,—we meaſure back the ſelf ſame ſteps
That we have trod before.

KILMALLOCK.

Faith, Count, then this falls out according to
my old luck. How hard it is upon induſtrious
travellers who follow their noſes on a journey, to
find out they have only been walking backwards
after all.—If the world do go round, as they ſay,
certain it has taken a twiſt extraordinary in the
night; elſe, the two ſides of the mountain could
never have fairly changed places.

VIROLET.

Droop not, Zorayda—~~let not the croſſes~~
~~We meet with, on our way, diſhearten thee.~~
~~Theſe difficulties, ever make the ſweets~~
~~We labour for, when once attain'd, ſeem ſweeter.~~
I prithee be of comfort.

ZORAYDA.

I will ſtrive
To keep my heart from ſinking: yet theſe perils
Might ſhake a firmer ſpirit. As I ſlept,
I dream't my father came to me in wrath,
And held a dagger o'er me.

KILMALLOCK.

KILMALLOCK.

I feldom knew a woman go to fleep that fhe did not dream upon mifchief. ~~Of a truth, though, when a grim fellow flourifhes his dagger before the clofed eyes of a lady, it muft make her lye a little uneafy.~~—Well, 'tis no wonder we have, at laft, loft our road; for the devil of any thing like one is there in this whole abominable Sierra de Ronda.

VIROLET.

Yon rock, which rifes in a rugged fpire,
O'er topping his bleak fellows, does appear
The mountain's utmoft fummit. Could we climb it,
Perchance, we might defcry fome diftant town,
To ferve us, as a beacon, on our way.

KILMALLOCK.

By my foul, now, you have hit on't. What an advantage it is to a head to be gifted with brains. I had ponder'd all day ere I had ftumbled on fuch an expedient—which carries with it only one fmall objection.

VIROLET.

What is't, Kilmallock?

KILMALLOCK.

'Tis fo fteep and perpendicular, that old Satan himfelf could never get up.

VIROLET.

Tut, man, I warrant—we'll affift each other.

KILMALLOCK.

Faith, and that's true again:—but I defy any human creature living to mafter it alone, but a cat or a monkey.

M VIROLET.

VIROLET.

Sure nought can harm her here—sweet, rest
  awhile :
Straight we will both return;—and bring, I trust,
The clue to wind thee (ere the sun has set)
From this same briary labyrinth.

ZORAYDA.

I pray you,
Wander not far, now,—when I am alone,
I shall turn coward here.

VIROLET.

Nay, nay, be patient.
'Tis for thy good, or sooth I would not leave thee.
Come honest comrade, and I swear to thee,
On a rough soldier's word, I know not how
E'er to requite thy friendship.

KILMALLOCK.

Pish, Count! what for scrambling up a rock!
---when I was a green-horn I would have gone
as far after a bird's nest.---O! Saint Iago! may
the man that faulters to risk his neck for a friend,
and a female, in a mountain, break it while he's
a boy climbing for eggs in an orchard!
           (Exeunt Virolet and Kilmallock.)

ZORAYDA.

I know not why it is, at this our parting,
My blood should flow so chilly thro' my veins!
'Tis not fatigue ;—for I have slept.—Is't fear?
Sure no—for I do now most firmly trust
There is a Power to throw its sacred shield
Before the zealous follower of its laws,
And ward off every danger.—I will rest me
                               'Till

'Till they come back again—for there is something,
Strange and unwonted, weighs upon my spirit,
'Till my weak body totters. *(Rests on a bank.)*

Enter BULCAZIN MULEY.

BULCAZIN.

Curses on them——
Fortune has pour'd her dregs of malice on me,
And pack'd these weak and halting knaves together
To check my expedition.—Ev'ry Moor
Measures his swarthy length upon the ground:
Beneath each bush there lies a fainting soldier.
That Ganem too should drop!—O! could I blow
One spark of a wrong'd father's rage among them,
The lusty band would march the world about,
As vigorously as the mountain deer
Will bound away a league. Still I will forward.
Should I o'ertake the changeling plodding, now,
Her way, with this same Christian runagate,
Were every limb unstrung with lassitude,
I think the loathsome sight would nerve my arm
To strike her dead before me. Soft! by Mahomet!
'Tis she!—Alone too—she seems weak and sinking.
O, my poor child!—my stubborn, wayward child!
Shame on't!—I shall forget my injuries——
Zorayda!——

ZORAYDA *(rising.)*
O heaven and earth!—my father!

BULCAZIN.
Aye—look on me—thou can'st not—well that's
something—

There

There still is left some touch of shame within
    thee—
Tell me, thou viper—what is't choaks me thus?
Oh! thou haft broke thy poor old father's heart.
My curses on thee! thy ingratitude,
Thy infamy—what made thee fly me?

           ZORAYDA.

  Conscience——
The holy zeal that led me from thy house
Burns high within me, now:—that frown, my
    father,
Would kill me else.—'Tis true I am your child!—
Stab me—I'll kiss the hand that gives me death—
But I would languish ages out in torture,
Ere I would quit that heaven-directed path,
The strong resistless movements of my soul
Do bid me follow.

           BULCAZIN.

Why 'tis bravely said.
Down passion, down—our parley shall be brief—
One point, and I have done. Tell me, Zorayda:—
I'd have it from thy lips—for circumstance
May hang a doubt upon't—and tell me true—
Is there a —— pshaw! I cannot utter it:—
Haft a companion in thy flight?

           ZORAYDA.

  My father,
I should disgrace the faith I follow now,
To utter falsehood to thee. There is One
Whose form and gallant bearing I confess,
Captur'd my maiden fancy, he has stray'd
Across this mountain with me: Yet, I swear,
My thought is not so loose and idly bent
To dwell on outward show. I had ne'er follow'
    him,

Had he not prov'd himself well-school'd in honour,
And a right Christian.

BULCAZIN.

Pestilence and torture!
Dost own it, wretch? Thou hast disgrac'd in thee
Thy father's blood; and justice, which has slept,
Now rouses, and will shed it.
(Offers to kill her.)

Enter OCTAVIAN, FLORANTHE, *and* ROQUE. *with his sword drawn.*

OCTAVIAN.

Ruffian, hold!
Advance thy arm the tythe part of an hair
To injure helpless woman, by my soul,
(Prove but my weapon true) thy turban'd head
Shall roll a trunkless ball upon the ground,
For crows to peck at.

BULCAZIN.

Busy fools, begone!
Ye do seem Christian—and it shocks my sight
To look on any of your tribe—get hence—
Nor cross a father's vengeance on his child.
I could have pardon'd her, had she not stoop'd
To mingle with thy herd—but she has fled
Our holy prophet's laws—fled, like a wanton,
To wander with a dog of thy persuasion.

OCTAVIAN.

Love and religion mingled! brighter flames
Ne'er glow'd within a virgin beauty's bosom:
And thou would'st smother them.—Thou'rt a
     true father!
Wretch!— the savage spirit that gives
     strength

To

To twenty thoufand Moors now brace thy finews,
I'd grapple with thee, thus, nor quit my hold
'Till I had offer'd thee a facrifice
On injur'd Love's pure altar.
*(They grapple —Octavian overthrows
Bulcazin Mulcy.)*

ZORAYDA.

O heaven! my father—my dear father, fave him.—

Enter VIROLET *and* KILMALLOCK.

VIROLET.

Zorayda—her father—ftop thy hand—
'Twere better thou didft plunge thy weapon here,
Home to my very heart, than let it fall
On him thou haft o'erthrown.—By heav'n, it is
The loft Octavian!

OCTAVIAN.

Thy word can charm me.
Thou art Floranthe's brother—and I fwear
For no man elfe could I reftrain the tranfport
That gufhes on my foul, when I have pull'd,
At laft, one flinty father to my feet,
Who tears the bands of virtuous love afunder,
And ftrews his children's path with thorns.
(Gives the fcymetar to Virolet.*)*

VIROLET *(to* Bulcazin*)*.

Sir, this which I reftore into your hand,
I fear me, in my abfence, has been rais'd
(Receive it now) againft a daughter's life:
He for whofe fake you would bereave her of it
Is bred in Chriftian faith—and it does teach him
To fhelter yours; and, in the hour of anguifh,
To offer fuccour to his enemy.

KILMALL.

ή Ζοrayda χ το Bulcazin

KILMALL.

Spoke, Count, like a noble gentleman. O, let a Chriſtian alone for a good action—he'll do you twenty in a breath without preaching—when a Muſſelman will ſhut up his Koran to go kick his fellow-creatures about like a parcel of foot-balls.

BULCAZIN.

Chriſtian, it ſeems I owe my life to thee;
'Tis a vaſt debt that thou haſt heap'd upon me,
And I have now a ſomething working here
Does urge me to requite thee—Truſt me, Chriſtian,
The rough and duſky boſom of a Moor
Does carry feeling in it.—My Zorayda,
My child, come hither to me—O this ſtruggle!
Zorayda, thy mother once was Catholick—
Her nature haply riſes in thee—Well,
I ſee 'twere vain to check it.—Take her, Chriſtian,
But ſpeak not to me now—my heart is full.
I will as far as Ronda with thee—there
We may confer more calmly.

ZORAYDA.

O, my father!

VIROLET.

This is a gift indeed!

KILMALL.

O, it does a man good to ſee kindneſs ſtealing into the breaſt of a Muſſelman! I fancy a Moor's heart isn't much prone to melting—but when once it begins, faith it keeps giving way by degrees, like a cold thaw.

FLORANTHE.

And now our toſſing paſſions have a pauſe,
Here let me greet a brother.

VIROLET.

VIROLET.

~~Can it be!
Floranthe here, and thus too!~~

BOQUE.

~~Aye, by my faith, my young master, we are all
met—and a cross dance we have had on't to
bring us together—but, my old heart bounds at
the meeting.~~

VIROLET.

My sister, ~~and Octavian too!~~ *But* ~~'tis strange!~~
How comes this?

FLORANTHE.

By your patience, gentle brother:
'Tis a long ~~tale we must deliver thee.~~
Yours we would know too—as we journey on,
We will discourse upon't—Mean time, be sure
Our travel ends in peace and honour.

~~VIROLET.~~

~~Prove
But this, Floranthe, ev'ry way I'm blest.~~

~~FLORANTHE.~~

~~Rest satisfied.~~

(Enter SADI *and* AGNES*).*

SADI.

Nay, come on, Agnes—With thee under one
arm, and a flagon under t'other, a fig for mountains, and let the world wag.

AGNES.

Mercy, here's a goodly company!—The Lady
Zorayda—O happy day!

SADI.

SADI.

And my old master, the Moor, by all the saints in Christendom!

VIROLET.

Peace, honest fellow, now thou meet'st all friends;
Let that content you.

SADI.

An' a man be not content when he meets all friends, I know not what will satisfy him—and that friends may not sunder again, here come a whole posse of goatherds at our heels going our road towards the foot of the mountain.

OCTAVIAN.

Then let us on; and when the shepherd tunes
His rustick pipe along the mountain's side,
We will beguile the way as we recount
Each turn that Fortune in her sport has mark'd,
As she has led us thro' Love's labyrinth.

(Enter Goatherds and other Pastoral Characters, male and female).

FINALE.

As we Goatherds trudge along,
O'er the mountain bleak and brown,
Merrily we troll the song,
Till we reach the distant town;

With scrip, and wine that sparkling smiles,
The dreary journey each beguiles;
Thro' cold and heat, thro' sun, thro' snow,
We sing, to market as we go.

CHORUS.

As we goatherds, &c.

Ser d²r.
: And each, a female by his side,
(Wedded wife, or wish'd-for bride,)
Cheerily descends the dale,
Whisp'ring soft a true-love tale.

CHORUS.
As we goatherds, &c.

Agnes.
Blest be ev'ry faithful pair!
May no rigid fires controul
In the bosoms of the fair
The pure emotions of the soul!

CHORUS.
Thus we goatherds, &c.

THE END.

NEW PLAYS, printed for J. DEBRETT, opposite Burlington-House, Piccadilly.

THE TRAVELLERS IN SWITZERLAND, a Comic Opera, by Mr. Bate Dudley, 1s. 6d.

The BOX-LOBBY CHALLENGE, a Comedy, by Richard Cumberland, Esq. 1s. 6d.

The WORLD IN A VILLAGE, a Comedy, by John O'Keefe, Esq. 1s. 6d.

The LONDON HERMIT, a Comedy, by John O'Keefe, Esq. 1s. 6d.

The ROAD TO RUIN, a Comedy, by Thomas Holcroft, Esq. 1s. 6d.

The FUGITIVE, a Comedy, by Joseph Richardson, Esq. 1s. 6d.

The HEIRESS, a Comedy, by Lieut. Gen. Burgoyne, 1s. 6d.

FALSE APPEARANCES, a Comedy, by the Right Hon. General Conway, 1s. 6d.

The FARM HOUSE, a Comedy, as altered by J. P. Kemble, Esq. 1s.

MARY, QUEEN of SCOTS, a Tragedy, by the Hon. John St. John, 1s. 6d.

L'ECOLE de SCANDALE, ou Les Mœurs du Jour, Comedie, par M. Sheridan. Traduite en Françoise par M. Bunel de Lille, Avocat au Parlement de Paris, 2s. 6d.

The ISLAND of ST. MARGUERITE, an Opera, 1s.

ALL'S WELL THAT ENDS WELL, a Comedy, written by Shakespeare, with alterations, by J. P. Kemble, Esq. 1s. 6d.

The TEMPEST, or the ENCHANTED ISLAND, written by Shakespeare, with additions from Dryden as compiled by J. P. Kemble, Esq. 1s. 6d.

KING HENRY V. or the CONQUEST OF FRANCE, a Tragedy, written by Shakespeare, printed exactly conformable to the Representation on its Revival at the Theatre Royal, Drury Lane, 1s. 6d.

RICHARD CŒUR DE LION, from the French of M. Sedaine, 1s. 6d.

The FAMILY PARTY, a Comic Piece, in Two Acts, 1s.

The LITTLE HUNCHBACK, or a FROLIC IN BAGDAD, by John O'Keeffe, Esq. 1s.

ALL

CATALOGUE OF PLAYS.

ALL IN GOOD H(J. 'OUR, a Dramatic Piece, 1s.
The ENCHANTED WOOD, a Legendary Dra[m]
Three Acts, 1s. 6d.
JUST IN TIME, a Comic Opera, by T. Hurlftone,

A SELECTION of feveral of the above much ef[teemed]
DRAMATIC PIECES, elegantly printed in two vols.
containing the HEIRESS, RICHARD CŒUR DE L[ION]
FALSE APPEARANCES, LITTLE HUNCHBAC[K]
TEMPEST, ISLAND OF ST. MARGUERITE, M[ARY]
QUEEN OF SCOTS, KING HENRY V. ALL'S \[WELL]
THAT ENDS WELL, JUST IN TIME, and the F[UGI]
TIVE: price 6s. in boards.

www.ingramcontent.com/pod-product-compliance
Lightning Source LLC
Chambersburg PA
CBHW022135160426
43197CB00009B/1296